Staying Strong in Unsteady Times

By Ray Hoskins, Beaconway Editions

A practical guide to staying clear, connected, and capable when life, politics, health, money, work, family, loss, or fear makes ordinary coping harder. Written for readers who are paying attention and feeling the cost of it. It tells the truth without leaving the reader alone with it.

Paperback ISBN 979-8-9934860-6-2
Beaconway Editions · First edition, 2026

Contents

Table of Contents

Introduction

Why I Wrote This Book

Before this book asks you to try any tool, I want you to know where I am writing from and what kind of help this is meant to be.

I learned early that the world can change in a day. I was fourteen when President John F. Kennedy was assassinated. Like many Americans, I watched the adults around me struggle to make sense of something that felt impossible the day before. I did not have the words for it then. I only knew that something stable had shifted.

In April 1968, Dr. Martin Luther King Jr. was killed. By then, the fracture did not feel abstract. It felt like part of the world I was growing up inside. Two months later, in June, Robert F. Kennedy was killed.

I had volunteered for his campaign and met him about three weeks before his death. I still remember the hope around that campaign. I also remember the shock after his death. Those years did not make me chronically afraid. They did teach me something I have never forgotten.

Instability is not theory. It happens.

When it happens, ordinary people have to figure out how to stay steady inside it. That question stayed with me.

Later, I studied history, political science, sociology, and economics. I trained to teach those subjects. Early in my career, I worked in urban education and community settings where large systems were not distant ideas. They were daily life. They shaped housing, schools, work, safety, opportunity, and dignity.

Over time, my work moved toward psychology, addiction treatment, counseling, coaching, and organizational change. The setting changed. The pattern did not.

Across those settings, one pattern kept returning. Power can be used with people, for people, or over people. When power is used over people, it does more than make decisions. It forces other human beings to live within choices they did not make. It can take away safety, dignity, predictability, and voice.

When people feel caught inside forces larger than themselves, their thinking narrows. Their bodies react. Their sense of clarity begins to erode. Sometimes they blame themselves for that.

They should not.

The human system was not built to carry endless threat, endless noise, endless cruelty, and endless uncertainty without cost.

This book grew out of that recognition. It is written for people who are paying attention and feeling the cost of paying attention. It is for people trying to stay decent while harm keeps coming.

It is for people grieving their country, their community, their safety, or a future they thought was more secure. It is for people who want to remain clear, grounded, and useful without pretending the weight is light.

I also need to say plainly where I am writing from now.

I am seventy-six years old. I have spent most of my life trying to live with restraint, compassion, fairness, and nonviolence. I have tried to understand people. I have tried not to let anger become hatred.

And still, in this season, I have felt anger I have rarely felt in my life.

Not ordinary irritation. Not political disappointment. Anger that surprises me.

Anger that scares me. Heaviness that is there before the day has fully begun.

Sometimes the anger flashes into thoughts I do not want to build a life around. Thoughts that confuse the urgent need to stop harm with a fantasy that the harm could simply disappear. I am not proud of those thoughts.

I am also no longer willing to pretend that decent people are not having thoughts like that.

For me, this has become part of the daily fight. I want to see clearly without drowning. I want to stay nonviolent without becoming passive. I want to care without pretending I am calm.

Most of all, I want to keep anger attached to protection, dignity, and life.

I also need to say one harder thing.

Anger is not always the only word.

There are moments when what I feel toward President Trump and this administration is hate.

I do not write that lightly. I have spent most of my life trying not to live from hate. I know what hate can do to a person from the inside.

But this hate does not begin with simple dislike. Without the power and the daily harm, he might only be a despicable man I could turn away from.

The hate comes because he is not private. He is the President of the United States. His administration has the power to harm people through law, money, force, fear, silence, and delay.

People are being harmed. Institutions are being damaged. Truth is being attacked. The climate is being damaged. The future is being made more dangerous. Each day can bring some new threat, cut, cruelty, lie, or attack on basic rights and dignity.

That is the place where many readers may be living too.

This book will not ask you to make that feeling smaller just so the page sounds polite. It will ask a better question:

How do we keep hate from taking more from us than the harm has already taken?

This book is not therapy. It is not legal, medical, crisis, or security advice. It cannot replace another person when you need one, and it should not become another demand placed on an already overloaded reader.

What it can offer is a practical frame for staying human under pressure.

We will focus strongly on helping you maintain a sense of "coherence". The theories at the base of much of this book state that coherence may be the most important resistance resource of all the ones that will be listed. Perhaps more important than safety, money, community, law, culture, rest, or practical help. Those resources matter deeply. I focus on coherence because it helps you keep enough of yourself together to recognize and use whatever resources are still within reach.

One of my sources, Aaron Antonovsky noticed that people do better under stress when life still feels somewhat understandable, when resources seem available, and when effort still has meaning. In plain language, coherence is the felt sense that:

- I can understand enough.
- This still matters.
- I can do something.

That is why disinformation, misinformation, and propaganda belong in this discussion. They do not only spread false claims. They can make reality harder to understand, trustworthy help harder to recognize, and shared meaning harder to sustain.

Some false information spreads because people are mistaken. Some is deliberately pushed to confuse, exhaust, divide, or demoralize. Either way, a thoughtful person can end the day feeling chaotic, suspicious, and unsure of their judgment.

That feeling is not proof that something is wrong with you. It may be evidence that the conditions for coherence and wellness are being eroded.

That may sound small until sustained pressure begins to strip it away. Repeated harm does not only create problems outside you. It can begin to invade your inner life. You may feel outrage, helplessness, and the daily harm. And the person(s) causing harm can start to feel like they own the center of your mind.

Coherence is the work of keeping your own center. You may still be angry. You may still be grieving. You may still be at risk. But you have not surrendered the link between reality, values, resources, and action.

This matters most when other sources of resistance are weakened. Many people cannot count on stable institutions, trusted cultural answers, legal protection, economic security, reliable healthcare, or a community that already knows how to respond. When those supports are damaged or out of reach, coherence may help a person find the next available support, borrow strength from another person, build a new answer, or refuse to let harm define the whole self.

That is why this book is not built around a single calming tool. It is built around the broader work of maintaining self and health under pressure. A person can lose many forms of support and still function if they can maintain enough coherence to say: "I know what I am seeing. I know what I value. I know I still belong to life. I can look for the next resource, the next ally, the next action, or the next place to rest."

That is not a minor matter. Under repeated abuse of power, maintaining that inner thread can be the most important act of resistance.

You do not need perfect calm to begin. You do not need perfect hope. You need a next place to stand. That is what this book offers.

It is not a book about denial. It is not a book about peace at any price. It is about protecting what is life-giving. It is about finding enough steadiness to keep choosing your values even as the world around you tries to choose for you.

This revision begins from that place.

Amid the heaviness. Still choosing life. Still trying to protect what matters. Still seeking the next right step.

Start Here

Start Here: How To Use This Book

Readers come to this book from different places. You may be holding up better than you expected and looking for something more useful than what you already have. You may be worn down from trying to stay decent while harm keeps coming. You may be angry in a way that surprises you. You may be grieving losses that others still refuse to name.

Some days, you may be watching for threats that were not present or did not feel this close when this book began. This book will not ask you to pretend the weight is smaller than it is. It will help you carry the weight without being crushed by it or letting it dictate every decision.

If possible, read the book in order first. The sequence matters. It begins with the frame, then moves through feelings, anger, hate, and helplessness, body tools, information, concrete risk, meaning, support, strategy, daily practice, and the long game. Later chapters break that work into smaller pieces so no single chapter has to carry too much weight.

That order is not accidental. Each part preserves one piece of coherence.

You may not be able to read in order today. That is fine. This book also offers help for the first few minutes, when your body or mind is flooded. It offers help for the long strain, when you are tired but still trying to keep going. It offers help for concrete risk, when safety, rights, work, family, medical care, immigration, identity, housing, speech, or community may be at stake.

Use the book in the way that fits your state today.

The Aim of the Book

Before this book asks you to maintain coherence, it needs to spend some time helping you understand what coherence means.

Many readers are not starting from a calm place. They are trying to regain enough clarity to know what is real, enough meaning to remember what matters, and enough support to choose the next step. So the first aim is not to ask you to guard a steady state you may not yet feel. Instead, it is to help you notice what has been strained, protect what remains, and rebuild one piece at a time.

Coherence does not mean pretending everything is fine.

It means staying connected to enough reality, meaning, support, and action so that pressure does not dictate every decision for you.

In plain words, coherence sounds like this:

- I can understand enough.
- This still matters.
- I can do something.

Those sentences may look simple. Under pressure, they can become hard to reach.

When coherence breaks down, everything gets harder.

- Facts blur.
- Feelings run the room.
- Danger may be minimized or exaggerated. Values may be replaced by panic, rage, shame, or numbness.
- The next step disappears.

Some of that break happens inside the body. Some of it is pushed at us from the outside.

A flood of distorted claims, threats, alarms, and cruelty can leave even a clear-headed person feeling scattered. It can prompt someone to ask: Why do I feel so chaotic? Why cannot I hold a steady thought?

Why can't I trust my own judgment today?

One answer is that coherence is being strained.

Sometimes it is worn down by overload. Sometimes it weakens from false information, humiliation, blame-shifting, sudden rule changes, or pressure to doubt what you see. The answer is not to shame yourself for it. The answer is to build pathways back.

One doorway question can help you before you choose a tool:

What does this moment require?

It may require settling your body for three minutes. It may require checking safety. It may require reducing demand, restoring a resource, asking another person for help, finding current information, taking one rightsized action, or resting before you break. The answer can change from day to day, even within the same day.

Then the three coherence questions help you move.

- What is happening?
- What matters?
- What can I do?

You do not need complete answers. You need enough of an answer to take one steadier step forward.

This is why coherence can matter even when other resources are weak. A person may still have a friend, a value, a useful fact, a public resource, a small skill, or a single possible action. But when coherence breaks, those resources can feel out of reach. You may not think to call the friend. You may not trust the useful fact. You may forget the value. You may not see the next step.

That is why this book offers more than calming techniques. Calming may help in the first few minutes, but it is not enough to sustain you under pressure. The deeper aim is to help you maintain enough coherence to use the resources you still have, build or borrow the resources you need, reduce demands where possible, and stay connected to yourself as pressure continues to mount.

This book is built like those pathways. If you still have coherence, it can help you protect it. If coherence is shaken, it can help you rebuild it, piece by piece. Sometimes the path back begins with the body. Other times, it begins with a reliable fact. Sometimes it begins with another person, a value, a boundary, a small action, or a place to rest.

The pieces of this book belong together:

- Safety checks and body tools help you regain your capacity.
- Feeling work helps you listen to your emotions without obeying every impulse.
- Hate and helplessness work helps you maintain moral clarity without letting the person causing harm become the center of your inner life.
- Information tools help you distinguish what needs action from what only consumes you.
- Concrete-risk tools help you respect danger without asking private coping to do work it cannot do.
- Demands and resources work helps you decide whether to reduce the load, restore a resource, or recruit help.
- Influence tools help you identify honest levers when control is unavailable.

Meaning, community, strategy, daily practice, and the long game help you rebuild and maintain coherence over time. Only now is maintaining coherence a fair aim. We are not pretending you begin with steadiness. We are practicing ways to return to it.

The aim is not endless calm. It is enough coherence to stay human, protect what matters, remember that you matter, and take the next right step.

You do not need all three parts fully back before you begin. You only need enough to take one steadier step.

First, Check Safety

If you are in immediate danger, this book is not the next step. Get to safety if you can. Contact someone you trust. Seek appropriate local emergency, crisis, medical, legal, or security help. If you are thinking about harming yourself, afraid you may harm someone else, or unable to keep yourself safe, do not try to handle it alone. In the United States, call or text 988 or use the 988 chat at https://988lifeline.org/chat/. Self-help is useful, but it is not a substitute for safety.

If you are in the United States, the Current Resources section includes crisis and safety starting points reviewed in this revision. If you are outside the United States, use the emergency, crisis, and safety resources available in your area.

Options For How To Use This Book

You can use this book in four ways.

Read it in order.

This is the best path if you have enough steadiness to do it.

Read the Introduction and the chapters in order. The book is designed to move from trust and orientation to inner steadiness, to hate and helplessness, to concrete risk, to meaning, community, strategy, daily practice, and the long game. Some chapters now pause or split the work to give the reader more room to absorb it.

Reading in order helps you see why the tools belong together. You are not just collecting techniques. You are building a way to restore coherence when pressure keeps coming, and then protect it as well as you can.

Use it for first help.

Start with Chapter Six, "Regaining Your Physiological Footing," when you need a few minutes to think clearly. The map below also points you to "Regaining Your Physiological Footing."

Use it for what you need today.

Use the section names below as doorways. This version directs you to the chapters where each topic receives greater attention.

Use it as a practice book.

Pick one activity, use it today, and stop there. You do not have to master the entire book to get help from one tool.

A Gentle Map of the Book

You do not need to know exactly what you need before you begin. Start with the place that sounds closest to your current state.

If Your Body or Mind Is Flooded applies for the first few minutes. The goal is not insight. It is enough steadiness to breathe, look around, name what is happening, and choose one next step.

See Chapter Six, "Regaining Your Physiological Footing," for more comprehensive body-based practices.

If You Are Worn Down and Trying to Keep Going, it is for the long haul. The goal is to stop running on alarm, guilt, or outrage alone. This path points toward meaning, support, and a sustainable lane.

See Chapter Nine, "The Question That Carries You Through," and Chapter Ten, "Rebuilding Meaning In Daily Life," for insight into meaning.

See Chapters Eleven and Twelve for support, and Chapters Thirteen and Fourteen for strategy.

If hate and helplessness are taking over, the book addresses the state many readers may not want to admit, even to themselves. The goal is not to shame hate or minimize the harm. The goal is to maintain moral clarity while finding one honest lever.

See Chapter Four, "When Hate Feels Honest"; Chapter Seven, "Managing The Information Flood"; and Chapters Thirteen and Fourteen for strategy.

If You Are Directly at Risk addresses concrete danger. The goal is protection, not private coping. This may involve safety, rights, work, family, medical care, immigration, identity, housing, speech, or community. See Chapter Eight, "When The Risk Is Concrete," and the Current Resources section near the end of the book.

If You Are Trying to Help Someone at Risk, it is helpful to do so without making the other person carry your fear. The goal is to provide concrete help, respect, privacy, and shared steadiness. See Chapters Eight, "When The Risk Is Concrete"; Eleven, "The Web That Holds You"; and Twelve, "Building And Protecting Your Web."

The Four Boxes is used to sort through too much information or too many pressures. The goal is to separate what needs action, preparation, help, or release. See Chapter Seven, "Managing The Information Flood."

When You Are Ready for the Deeper Frame helps you understand why the pieces fit together. The goal is to see how coherence, meaning, community, and right-sized action help people remain mentally and morally healthy under sustained pressure. Begin with Chapter One, "Finding Strength In Dark Times," then return to the later chapters as needed.

Chapter One: Finding Strength in Dark Times

How to Use This Chapter

Use this chapter when you are ready for the deeper frame underneath the tools. If your body is flooded or safety is at stake, begin with first help or current support and come back later. Here the main job is to understand coherence in plain language: what is happening, what matters, and what you can do. Let the chapter give you a map, not another demand.

The Frame Underneath the Tools

You already have the first tools.

You know how to check for safety. You know how to slow your breathing. You know how to find the room, name the feeling, and choose the next action.

Those tools matter because under pressure, strength does not begin with a big theory. It begins with getting enough of yourself back to take the next right step.

This chapter explains the frame underneath that work.

The frame is coherence.

Coherence means:

- I can understand enough.
- This still matters.
- I can do something.

When those three things are present, even imperfectly, people are better able to stay steady under strain.

When they are shaken all at once, people often feel confused, helpless, exhausted, angry, numb, or lost. That does not mean they are weak.

It means the load is touching the basic conditions people need to function.

The Three Questions

The practical form of coherence is simple.

Ask:

1. What is happening?
1. What matters?
1. What can I do?

You do not need perfect answers. You need enough of an answer to take one step forward.

What is happening? This is the question of understanding. It helps you sort out what you know, what you do not know, what you are feeling, what your body is doing, and whether there is real danger.

What matters? This is the question of meaning. It helps you remember what you are protecting, who you love, what value is at stake, and what kind of person you want to be.

What can I do? This is the question of agency. It does not mean you can control everything.

It means there may be one action, one preparation, one person to contact, or one thing to stop carrying.

These three questions are at the center of this book. The rest of the book keeps returning to them in different forms.

A Short Practice

This practice is here so the frame does not remain abstract. It helps you try coherence in the smallest possible form before you read more theory. Use it when you have enough steadiness to pause for one minute.

Ask three questions:

- What is happening? Write one honest sentence. It can be as simple as "I am flooded," "I am afraid," or "I do not know yet."
- What matters? Name one person, value, place, community, promise, or future you are trying to protect.

- What can I do? Name one step, one preparatory action, or one person who could help.

Do not try to make the answers impressive. The purpose is not insight for its own sake. It is to bring reality, meaning, and action back into the same room.

That is coherence beginning to return.

Not all at once. One honest answer at a time.

Coherence Under Stress

Coherence does not mean you are calm.

It means you are less lost.

Return to the three questions:

- What is happening?
- What matters?
- What can I do?

Under urgent pressure, the order may need to bend.

Ask:

1. What is happening?
2. What can I do right now?
3. What matters enough to protect?

Safety comes before reflection. If you or someone else is in immediate danger, seek help first. You can return to meaning later.

The point is not to think perfectly. It is to recover enough understanding, meaning, and agency to take the next right step.

Where This Frame Comes From

I did not invent the deeper idea of coherence. Two thinkers are especially important to this book.

Aaron Antonovsky was a medical sociologist who studied why some people were able to move toward health even after severe stress. Rather than asking only what makes people sick, he asked what helps people stay well.

That is why Antonovsky gives us the framework.

His question matters here because the readers of this book are not in a simple problem-solving moment. Many are living under repeated pressure. They may be watching harm unfold through politics, institutions, media, courts, policies, money, climate, and culture. They may not be able to stop the central harm today. In that kind of strain, the deeper question is not only How do I calm down? It is also How do I keep enough of myself to see clearly, stay connected to what matters, and make use of whatever help still exists?

That is the coherence question.

Mental health is not protected only by calming down. It is protected by maintaining enough coherence to remain clear, connected, and capable when pressure tries to scatter the self.

Antonovsky described coherence as having three parts:

- Comprehensibility: life makes enough sense that you are not lost in confusion.
- Manageability: you can find or build enough resources to meet the requirements.
- Meaningfulness: the effort still connects to something worth protecting.

These three parts do not make life easy.

They make life more possible.

When comprehensibility breaks down, people feel lost. They cannot tell what is true, what matters, what is changing, or what is being done to them. When manageability breaks, people feel trapped. They may see the problem clearly but believe they have no resources, no help, no lever, and no way to respond.

When meaningfulness breaks, people feel hollow. They may still understand the facts and know possible actions, but they lose contact with why the effort matters.

That is why coherence is not an abstract idea in this book. It is a resistance resource. More than that, it may be the resource that helps the other resources become usable. It helps protect the mind from confusion, helplessness, despair, and isolation.

Viktor Frankl was a psychiatrist who wrote about meaning after surviving Nazi concentration camps. His wife, parents, and brother did not survive. He wrote from scholarship, clinical training, and direct encounter with extreme suffering.

That is why Frankl gives us part of the meaning thread.

His work reminds us that human beings need more than relief from pain. We need reasons to keep choosing life, dignity, love, responsibility, and purpose when circumstances are hard.

These two sources do different work here.

Antonovsky helps explain coherence.

Frankl helps explain why meaning matters when life is hard.

Antonovsky's answer centered on a sense of coherence: the felt sense that life is at least somewhat understandable, that resources are available, and that effort still has meaning.

This book translates coherence into plain language:

- I can understand enough.
- This still matters.
- I can do something.

The point is not that our situation is comparable to the camps Frankl survived.

It is not.

The point is that Frankl's work helps us respect meaning as a real human need under severe strain.

Frankl And Meaning

Frankl had already begun developing his ideas about meaning before the Nazis arrested him in 1942. Over the next three years, he was held in several concentration camps.

His manuscript was taken from him. Later, he reconstructed his work and wrote about what he had witnessed.

We need to use Frankl carefully.

Meaning is not a survival formula. No one should use meaning to judge people crushed by violence, starvation, illness, terror, or chance.

The safer claim is this: meaning can help people endure, remain answerable to love, and protect dignity when control is limited.

Frankl described three pathways to meaning:

- Creative meaning: what we give to the world through work, service, care, art, repair, or contribution.

- Experiential meaning: what we receive from the world through love, beauty, truth, nature, music, friendship, and moments of grace.
- Attitudinal meaning: how we face suffering that cannot yet be changed, without pretending it is good.

That last point matters in this book. Some things can be changed and should be fought for. Some things cannot be changed today. Even then, we can ask who we want to be while we face them.

Antonovsky And Resources

Antonovsky gives us another piece of the map.

Health is not simply present or absent. People move along a continuum. Some things push us toward illness, exhaustion, despair, and collapse. Other things help us move toward health, strength, clarity, and connection.

He called many of those supports Generalized Resistance Resources. In plain language, these are resources that help across many kinds of stress. They can include:

- Physical supports, such as sleep, food, movement, medical care, and basic physical strength.
- Practical supports, such as money, housing, transportation, records, and access to services.
- Knowledge, such as understanding what is happening and where to find reliable help.
- Emotional capacity, such as the ability to pause, name a feeling, and not let the first impulse make the choice.
- Values and beliefs, such as knowing what kind of person you are trying to be.
- Relationships, such as friends, family, neighbors, groups, and people who can help you think or act.
- Culture and institutions, such as shared answers, trusted places, community habits, and systems that still protect people.
- Coping strategies, such as the tools in this book.You do not need all of these to be strong before you begin. No one has all of them all the time.

The list matters because stress does not ask politely which resources you still have. It may attack sleep, money, safety, community, culture, and hope at once. Under that kind of pressure, coherence helps you ask a better question than, Why am I not handling this better?

The question is simpler:

What resource can I notice, restore, build, or borrow right now?

That question matters because people under stress often blame themselves for lacking more control. Sometimes the problem is not a matter of character. Sometimes the problem is a lack of resources.

That does not leave us helpless. It shows us where to build. It also shows why coherence matters so much. If you can still ask where a resource might be found, borrowed, restored, or created, you have not lost the thread.

How Coherence Grows and Breaks

Antonovsky did not treat coherence as a fixed trait that some people have and others lack. Coherence grows or weakens through lived experience.

It grows when life is consistent enough to make sense. It grows when the load is heavy but not beyond available resources. It grows when people have meaningful participation in the decisions that affect them. Later work also underscores the importance of emotional closeness, because people usually hold together better when they are not isolated.

That helps explain why this period is so destabilizing. When rules change suddenly, comprehensibility is undermined. When institutions, rights, benefits, medical care, work, safety, or money become less reliable, manageability is undermined. When people feel that decisions about their lives are being made without their voices mattering, meaningfulness is undermined.

Information can weaken coherence too. Misinformation may spread because people are mistaken. Disinformation and propaganda are often used to influence people on purpose. The effect can be the same in the reader's mind.

Reality becomes harder to discern. Trust becomes harder to place. Shared meaning becomes less stable. A person does not only think: I disagree with this. They may begin to think: I cannot tell what is real, who can help, or what matters anymore.

That is one way coherence gets sabotaged.

This is not only a private mental health issue. It is one reason authoritarian pressure is so damaging. It does not only threaten policies or programs. It threatens the conditions people need to think clearly, act with agency, and remain connected to what gives life meaning.

The answer is not to pretend we control what we cannot control. The answer is to rebuild coherence wherever we can: in the body, in information, in resources, in relationships, in shared action, in culture, and in the next faithful step.

Meaning Is the Engine

Antonovsky treated meaningfulness as central because people are more likely to draw on their understanding and resources when the effort feels worthwhile. If nothing matters, even good tools can sit unused. If something matters deeply, people often find the energy to learn, connect, prepare, and act.

This is where Antonovsky and Frankl meet. Frankl helps us see why meaning can keep people answerable to life under severe strain. Antonovsky helps us see how meaning, together with understanding and resources, supports health. Together, they point toward the same practical truth:

You need more than calm. You need a reason, a map, and resources you can access.

Why This Matters Now

Many people are not only upset but also disoriented right now.

They are trying to understand what is happening as the information keeps changing. They are trying to act even as the scale of the problems feels too large.

They are trying to keep caring as outrage, fear, grief, and exhaustion take turns.

That is why coherence matters. The goal is not to pretend that everything is fine.

The goal is to regain enough understanding, agency, and meaning to stay human and take the next right step.

The chapters that follow will repeatedly return to the same three needs:

- Comprehensibility: seeing clearly enough to respond.
- Manageability: finding and building real resources.
- Meaningfulness: staying connected to what makes effort worth it.

You will not be asked to carry this alone. Individual steadiness matters, but it is not enough on its own.

The work ahead includes body tools, information tools, direct-risk tools, meaning tools, community tools, daily practice, and long-term practice.

A Simple Learning Pattern

When applicable, this book will use a simple learning pattern:

1. Identify.
2. Analyze.
3. Generalize.

Identify means naming what is happening in plain words. What am I feeling? What changed? What is the risk? What is loudest right now?

Analyze means asking what the pattern is telling you. Is this about danger, grief, overload, violated values, missing resources, isolation, or a need for action? What does this moment require?

Generalizing means carrying the learning forward. Where else does this pattern appear? What helped? What would I want to remember next time? Could this also help someone else?

This keeps the book from becoming a list of techniques. A tool helps once. A pattern helps you learn to keep helping yourself and others.

What Comes Next

Before we move to the next chapter, take a moment to ground yourself.

You do not need a quiet afternoon or a perfect journal. You only need a few honest minutes. The point is to leave this chapter with one small mark on the map: how clear things feel, which resources you can still access, and what matters enough to protect.

Take five minutes if you can.

Before You Move On

Ask three questions.

1. Comprehensibility

On a scale of one to ten, how well do you understand what is happening in your world right now?

Include more than politics. Include your relationships, your body, your local situation, and your sense of what may be coming.

Write the number down. Do not explain it yet. Just record it.

2. Manageability

What resources are available to you at the moment?

Think of people, knowledge, practical support, physical support, and inner strengths.

Most of us, even when depleted, undercount our resources. Write down three you have, even if they feel small.

3. Meaningfulness

What are you doing any of this for?

Not a complete answer. A starting point.

Name one person, value, place, community, or future that matters enough to protect.

Keep these answers somewhere. You will return to them.

Chapter Two: Your Feelings Are Information

How To Use This Chapter

Use this chapter when a feeling is loud and you are unsure how to handle it. Fear, anger, grief, shame, numbness, and exhaustion can all carry information. They may point to danger, a violated value, a loss, an old wound, or an excessive load. The purpose here is not to make the feeling disappear. The purpose is to hear it clearly enough that it does not have to drive the whole car.

Your Feelings Are Information

Before we go further, try one small thing. Name what you are feeling.

Use ordinary words:

- Fear.
- Grief.
- Rage.
- Dread.
- Shame.
- Numbness.
- Confusion.
- Exhaustion. Too much.

You do not need the perfect word. The closest honest word is enough.

Say it simply:

- This is fear.
- This is grief.
- This is rage.
- This is shame.
- This is numbness. This is too much.

If two feelings are present, name both. This is fear and anger. This is grief and exhaustion. This is dread and love. Naming the feeling does not make it vanish. It gives you a little more room around it. It turns the feeling from the whole room into something you can notice, hold, and question.

Mike And Janet

Mike had always been the calm one. When trouble came, people called him. When family tension rose, he made peace. He coached kids without yelling. He helped neighbors fix things. Then he found himself sitting in a grocery store parking lot, his hands clamped on the wheel.

His heart was racing.

A clerk had said something that hit him harder than it should have. Later that week, he yelled at his daughter about the dishes in the sink. That was not like him. The worst moment came at a family gathering. A relative praised policies Mike believed would harm children in their own town. Mike felt his chest tighten. His hands clenched into fists.

He had to leave the room because he feared what he might say. That night, he told Janet, "I do not feel like myself." Janet understood. She had stopped attending gatherings, too. She had stopped watching movies because ordinary entertainment felt strange amid so much harm. Even her garden, her refuge for years, felt different. "I feel like I am living in another reality," she said.

"People talk about normal things while I watch our country come apart." Both were sleeping poorly, checking the news too often, and snapping at the people they loved.

Both wondered the same thing:

Are we falling apart? No. They were not falling apart. They were experiencing strong human reactions to sustained pressure. That does not mean every reaction was wise or that every impulse should be trusted. It means the feelings deserved attention.

Let The Feeling Speak Before It Drives

A feeling may be telling you something important. It may signal danger. It may signal a value being violated. It may signal grief, love, overload, or an old wound. Let it speak. Do not let it drive the whole car before you understand what it is carrying.

Ask one question:

What is this feeling trying to tell me?

Then, if you can, ask:

- Is there a concrete risk?
- Is something I love being threatened?
- Is a value being violated?
- Is my body overloaded?
- Do I need action, preparation, support, or rest?

Do not ask all of these at once. Choose the one that fits.

A Small Map of Common Feelings

This is not a complete list. Human beings have more reactions than a single chapter can hold. You only need enough of a map to begin listening.

- Fear may be asking you to pay attention. Something may be unsafe. You may need more information, another person's help, or a safer plan.
- Anger may be telling you that a value has been violated. Something or someone may need protection.
- Rage carries more heat. It may say, "This has to stop right now." Listen to the urgency. Do not hand it the whole decision. Let your values choose the means.
- Hate may be telling you that harm has become attached to a person, group, system, or movement in your mind. The harm may be real. The danger is that hate can make the target fill your entire inner world. It needs to be translated into protection, accountability, and action.
- Sadness and grief may be telling you that something you love has been wounded or lost. You can grieve a person, a

relationship, your country, or a future you believed was still possible. Grief is not a weakness. It is the mind and body honoring that something mattered.

- Overwhelm may mean that too much is arriving at once. Too much news. Too much danger. Too many decisions. Too many people needing help. Too little rest, support, or order. Overwhelm is not proof that you cannot cope.
- Dread may be saying, I can feel trouble coming, but I cannot yet see its exact shape. That may call for preparation. It may also call for a break from scanning. Shame may be saying, I am afraid I have failed or that I will be cast out. Shame often overclaims. It can confuse pain with guilt. It needs mercy and a trusted witness before it is believed.
- Numbness may mean the volume is too high. Sometimes numbness is not a lack of love. It is the human system lowering the volume.
- Exhaustion may mean the load has outpaced recovery. That is not a character flaw. It is information about limits.
- Love may be saying, "This is why I am still here." Do not miss that. Amid grief, anger, fear, and exhaustion, love is often still the ground.

Use the closest honest word. Then ask what it may be pointing toward.

Feelings Need Discernment

Feelings are information. They are not always the full picture. A feeling can point toward truth. It can also mix truth with exhaustion, old pain, fear, habit, too much news, or too little rest. That does not make the feeling wrong. It means the feeling needs company. It needs evidence. It needs your values. It may need another person. The question is not whether the feeling is valid. The question is what the feeling needs you to notice.

Unhook from the Loudest Thought

Some thoughts arrive with a voice of certainty.

- Nothing will get better.
- I cannot handle this. Everyone is unsafe.
- I have already failed. This will never end.

When a thought is that loud, it can feel like a fact. It may contain real information, but it may also contain fear, exhaustion, old pain, or too much news.

The work is not to fight the thought. It is to unhook from it long enough to choose.

Put these words in front of the thought:

I am having the thought that...

For example:

- I am having the thought that nothing will ever get better.
- I am having the thought that I cannot handle this.
- I am having the thought that everyone is unsafe.

If the thought still has you by the throat, try saying: A part of me is saying...

This does not make the thought silly. It makes it smaller than your whole self.

Do not use this to deny risk. If you are in danger, do not talk yourself out of it. Use this tool to think more clearly as you assess the risk with facts, support, and current information.

Then ask:

- What is this thought afraid of?
- What is it trying to prevent?
- What does it want me to notice?
- Does this call for action, preparation, connection, or parking for now?

A thought can be loud and still not be the whole truth.

When The Feeling Points to Danger

If the feeling points to a concrete risk, take it seriously. Do not talk yourself out of it just to feel calmer.

Ask:

- What do I know?
- What do I need to know?

- Who can help me assess this?
- Which current resources apply?
- What next step would make me safer?

Fear in the face of real risk is not a personal flaw. It is a signal for care, clarity, and support. If the answer is safety, do not treat it as private coping work. Get help if you can. Use current, reliable resources. Involve someone trustworthy when it is safe to do so.

Before You Move On

Try this once today.

Choose one feeling that is present.

Name it plainly.

Then ask three questions:

- What might this feeling be trying to tell me?
- Is it pointing to danger, a violated value, a loss, or too much load?
- What would help me take one steadier step?

You do not have to solve the feeling.

You only have to begin listening.

That is enough for now.

Chapter Three: When Anger Scares You

How To Use This Chapter

Use this chapter when your anger surprises or frightens you, especially if you have tried to live with restraint, compassion, tolerance, or nonviolence. The purpose is to name the anger without obeying it, then translate it into protection, dignity, and life-serving action. If anger has become planning, rehearsal, pursuit, access, or fear of hurting yourself or someone else, stop reading for now and get real-time help. Create distance, contact a trusted person, and use appropriate crisis or emergency support.

The Anger You Did Not Expect

Some anger feels familiar. You know what it is, why it came, and what to do with it. Then there is the other kind. The anger that arrives so suddenly that you feel almost afraid of yourself. The anger that flashes through your body before you have chosen a word.

The anger that makes a peaceful person think, for one terrible second, that they wish that person would die. If that has happened to you, this chapter is for you. Not because the thought is harmless in every situation. Not because anger is always wise.

Not because wishing harm on another human being is something to build a life on.

This chapter is here because many decent people are experiencing feelings they never expected to feel.

People who have spent their lives trying not to hate. People who believe in nonviolence. People who have worked to remain open, tolerant, humane, and fair-minded.

People who have repeatedly told themselves that they will not become what they oppose.

And still, the anger comes.

Sometimes it comes when you read one more story about cruelty treated as policy. Sometimes it comes when another institution fails to hold the line. Sometimes it comes when people laugh at suffering, excuse corruption, or make a game of fear. Sometimes climate alone is enough.

The damage is not a single event you can grieve and then leave behind.

It is daily and cumulative.

It touches children, elders, communities, animals, forests, oceans, seasons, homes, and futures. The harm keeps coming, and some of it was preventable.

A person who can see that and not feel anger may be shielded by distance, denial, exhaustion, or privilege.

A person who can see it clearly may feel the anger in the body before any philosophy has a chance to speak.

That does not make you bad. It means something in you still refuses to accept ongoing harm as normal.

Tolerance Was Never Meant to Mean This

Many readers of this book have tried to be tolerant. They have tried to listen. They have tried to keep relationships intact. They have tried to separate people from their worst opinions. They have tried to believe that conversation, patience, and decency can still matter. Those commitments are worth protecting. But tolerance was never meant to mean making peace with cruelty. Nonviolence was never meant to mean being without anger.

Compassion was never meant to mean letting harm pass through the world without protest. There is a kind of moral confusion that arises when people who value peace begin to feel violent anger. They look at the feeling and think, If this is in me, then maybe I have failed. That conclusion is too quick. A violent thought may mean many things. It may mean you are exhausted. It may mean your nervous system has been under pressure for too long.

It may mean your mind is grasping for the simplest image of an ending: if that person were gone, the harm would stop. It may mean you feel trapped between love for life and exposure to daily harm. It may mean your values are still alive, but your current tools are not enough. The thought is not the whole story. It is a signal. It deserves attention. It does not deserve command.

A Thought Is Not A Plan

One of the most important distinctions in this chapter is the difference between a thought and a plan.

A thought can arrive uninvited. A wish can pass through the mind and frighten you. An image can appear and make you recoil.

An urge can arise in the body and still not be something you choose.

A plan is different.

A plan begins to organize behavior. It gets rehearsed. It seeks opportunity. It moves toward access. It starts to feel justified. It becomes something you protect from interruption.

If you are having an unwanted thought that horrifies you, the first task is not to hate yourself. Instead, the first task is to name it accurately.

You can say:

I am having violent thoughts. I am having a death wish. I am having a revenge fantasy. I am not choosing violence. I need to understand what this anger is carrying.

That is very different from saying:

This is who I am. This is what I should do. This person deserves whatever happens. I have no choice. The first set of sentences creates space. The second set narrows that space. When the space narrows, get help widening it.

What The Anger May Be Carrying

Anger often carries a protest.

Something is wrong. Someone is being harmed. A boundary has been crossed. A value has been violated. A future is being stolen. That does not mean anger is always accurate in every detail.

It can misread a moment. It can latch onto the wrong target. It can turn a tired body into a courtroom and put the nearest person on trial.

But anger should not be dismissed merely because it is uncomfortable.

Ask what it is carrying.

- Is it carrying grief?
- Is it carrying fear?
- Is it carrying helplessness?
- Is it carrying love?
- Is it carrying the knowledge that someone is being hurt and you cannot make it stop?
- Is it carrying the strain of watching systems protect power while ordinary people and the living world pay the cost?

Sometimes the anger is so intense because the love underneath it is so large.

- Love for children. Love for the earth.
- Love for democratic life.
- Love for people whose safety is being negotiated by those who will not suffer the consequences.
- Love for truth.
- Love for a future that has not yet been fully lost.

If you only look at the anger, you may become afraid of yourself. If you listen beneath it, you may find the value that needs protection.

Anger And Rage

Anger tells you a value has been violated. Rage says the violation needs to stop. That is why rage can feel so different from ordinary anger. It carries urgency. It does not want understanding first. It wants interruption. It wants the harm ended now. Sometimes that urgency protects life.

If a child is in danger, if a person is being attacked, if someone is being abused, or if a community is being targeted, the body may not politely ask whether action is appropriate. It may rise up with force because something must be stopped. That is part of why rage can feel morally convincing. It is not merely heat. It is urgency attached to a violated value. But rage has a dangerous weakness. It does not naturally count the cost.

Rage may say:

Stop this, even if it destroys me. Stop this, even if it destroys them. Stop this, even if it destroys the work. Stop this, even if it hands my enemies the story they wanted. Stop this, even if I become less able to protect what I love. That is where the discipline begins. The discipline is not to deny the rage. The discipline is to refuse to let rage dictate the cost. Violence has consequences. It harms real bodies.

It creates grief that cannot be neatly directed only at the person you meant to harm. It can lead to legal consequences, retaliation, escalation, isolation, and loss of freedom. It can harm the people who depend on you. It can weaken the very movement, family, or community you were trying to protect. It can also change you.

The first act may be intended to stop harm, but violence rarely stays within the clean moral boundary the imagination gave it. It spills. It spreads. It teaches the nervous system a new answer. That does not mean there are no hard questions in history.

It means

that when rage says violence would solve the violation, you should slow the room down before accepting its math.

Ask:

- What value has been violated?
- What needs to stop?
- Who needs protection?
- What would stop harm without becoming the harm?
- What action would I still be willing to answer for tomorrow, next year, and in front of the people whose respect matters most to me?

Rage brings the urgency. Your values must choose the means.

The Death Wish

We need to speak plainly about this.

A person can oppose violence and still have a moment when they wish someone would die.

Often, the wish is not really a wish for death so much as a wish for the harm to stop. The mind reaches for the simplest ending it can imagine.

If that person were gone, this would end. If that voice fell silent, people would be safer. If that source of harm disappeared, I could breathe.

This is not a noble thought. It is also not a rare human thought.

The danger is not that such a thought passes through the mind. The danger is when the thought becomes a place you live in. When you feed it.

When you rehearse it. When you let it flatten another human being into nothing but the harm they represent. When you begin to believe that your relief matters more than your values. When you begin to seek out situations where harm could occur. That is where the boundary shifts. The nonviolent task is not to pretend the thought never came. The task is to translate it before it hardens.

Often the translation is:

I want the harm to stop. I want people protected. I want accountability. I want the systems that enable this to lose power. I want life to have a chance. These are different wishes. They can become action without turning violent.

Anger As Bait

There is another reason to take this seriously. Once your anger enters the public sphere, it is no longer yours alone. Media systems, political actors, and online platforms know that outrage captures attention. Outrage keeps you watching, clicking, sharing, and coming back. It can make you feel awake while slowly training your nervous system to live in a state of threat. This does not mean your anger is fake. It means your anger can be used.

Someone who wants you exhausted does not need to defeat your values. They only need to keep you so activated that your values cannot guide your behavior. Someone who wants you discredited does not need you to become violent. They only need you to speak or act from your most flooded state.

Someone who wants democratic people to look dangerous benefits whenever a person committed to justice is baited into dehumanizing speech, reckless action, or public contempt that confirms the other side's narrative. This is why anger needs care, not suppression. Anger is powerful. Powerful things need direction.

The Nonviolent Question

When anger scares you, the question is not:

How can I stop being angry?

The better question is:

How do I keep this anger focused on protection, dignity, and life?

That question matters because anger can move in multiple directions.

It can move toward:

- Revenge.
- Contempt.
- Fantasy.
- Collapse.

It can also move toward:

- Protection.
- Organizing.
- Courage.
- Truth-telling.
- Disciplined resistance.
- Care for the people and places being harmed.

Your task is not emotional purity. Your task is direction.

A Short Practice: Translate The Anger

When anger frightens you, do not start with analysis. Start with interruption.

1. Stop.

Do not post. Do not send the message. Do not make the call. Do not confront the person. Do not drive toward the situation. Create a brief pause between anger and action.

2. Name it.

Use plain words. I am furious. I am afraid of my anger. I am having violent thoughts. I am wishing someone would disappear or die. I do not choose violence.

3. Ask what needs to stop.

Do not ask who deserves suffering.

Ask:

- What harm needs to stop?
- What is being done?
- Who is being hurt?
- What value is being violated?
- What future am I trying to protect?
- Choose a life-protecting action.

Pick one action that protects life, dignity, truth, community, or the future. It may be small. Contact one person. Give to one organization. Document one fact. Rest before you break. Join work already underway. Leave the argument. Prepare for the next useful step. The action does not have to match the size of the anger. It has to keep faith with the value beneath it.

When Anger Comes in Bursts

Some anger does not arrive as a clear moral judgment. It arrives as a burst. You snap at someone you love. You feel heat in your chest over a minor inconvenience. You slam a cabinet. You feel rage toward a stranger who did very little.

Then you are ashamed because the reaction seems too big for the moment. It probably is. That does not mean it came from nowhere. Under sustained pressure, the body stacks alarms. One more headline, one more policy, one more cruel joke, one more denial of reality, one more climate disaster, one more conversation with someone who seems untouched by the harm. The visible trigger may be small, but the load beneath it is not.

When anger bursts, ask:

- What did this moment touch? What was already in me before this happened?
- What have I been carrying without a place to put it?
- Who can help me slow this down?

Then repair what needs repair.

If you snapped at someone, say so.

If you frightened someone, own it.

If you broke trust, rebuild it.

Accountability is not the enemy of self-compassion. It is one way to keep your values intact.

If You Are Afraid Of Yourself

Take this seriously. Do not handle it alone. If you are afraid you may hurt yourself or someone else, if you are rehearsing harm, if you are seeking access to a person or situation, if substances are lowering your restraint, or if the thought is starting to feel like an instruction, create distance now. Get another person involved.

Contact a trusted friend, clinician, spiritual leader, community leader, crisis support, or appropriate local emergency support. If you are in the United States, call or text 988 or use the 988 chat at https://988lifeline.org/chat/. Asking for help does not prove you are bad. You are protecting your values even when the room is narrow. That is what nonviolence looks like under pressure. It is not the absence of anger.

It is the decision to build safeguards around anger before it can cause harm.

Before You Move On

Try this once before you leave this chapter. Write three sentences.

First:
The anger I am carrying is about:
Second:
The value underneath it is:
Third:
One life-protecting action I can take is:
If the anger is too hot to answer clearly, begin with the body.

- Exhale slowly.
- Find the room.
- Put both feet on the floor.
- Contact one steady person.

Then return to the three sentences.
You do not have to become less human to stay nonviolent.
You do not have to pretend daily harm is tolerable.
You do not have to be calm before you are allowed to care.
But you do need a way to keep anger connected to what it came to protect.
Protection. Dignity. Life.

Chapter Four: When Hate Feels Honest

How To Use This Chapter

Use this chapter if you feel more than anger. You may hate what a leader, administration, movement, or group of people using power cruelly is doing, and you may feel helpless because you cannot stop the harm today. The purpose is not to shame that truth or to soften the harm. The purpose is to keep hate from becoming the center of your inner life and to return your energy to protection, accountability, community, and one honest lever. If hate is turning into planning, rehearsal, pursuit, or fear that you may act violently, involve another person and use appropriate local help now.

The Word I Do Not Want to Need

I need to be honest about my starting point.

I do not feel only anger toward President Trump and this administration. At times, I feel hate.

That is not a sentence I like writing. I have spent most of my life trying not to live in hate. I believe in nonviolence, restraint, mercy, and accountability. I also believe in truth.

For me, the hate does not begin with ordinary dislike. Without the office, the power, and the daily harm, he might be only a despicable man I could turn away from. The hate comes because he is not private.

He holds power over real people. His administration can harm people through law, money, enforcement, fear, delay, and silence. That changes how people feel.

When cruelty is only personal, you may be able to leave the room. When it is tied to public power, the room follows people into their lives. It follows them into medical care, work, school, housing, identity, speech, benefits, safety, courts, weather, and the future their children may inherit.

That is why hate can begin to feel honest. Not noble. Not safe. Honest enough that pretending it is not there may only leave the reader feeling more alone.

When Hate and Helplessness Come Together

Hate by itself is dangerous. Hate plus helplessness is even more dangerous because the feeling has nowhere to go. It knows something is wrong, but it cannot find the lever to stop the harm.

Hate says:

"I see the harm."

Helplessness says:

"I cannot stop it."

Together, they can create a hard inner loop. You watch one more thing happen. One more threat. One more cut. One more lie. One more act of cruelty. One more person hurt. One more institution bending. One more danger to the climate, the country, or the world.

You look for a way to stop it now, but there may not be one. So the mind returns to the person at the center. It studies him, despises him, waits for consequences, imagines his removal, and searches for one more reason to confirm what it already knows.

That loop can feel like resistance. Sometimes it is merely captivity. Watching harm is not the same as resisting it. Knowing one more terrible thing is useful only if it helps you care, decide, plan, connect, protect, or act.

Hate Has Already Been Used As A Tool

There is another reason to be careful about hate. We are not meeting it in a neutral world.

For years, much political propaganda has invited people to hate the administration's opponents and the groups it targets.

Immigrants, trans people, racial and religious minorities, journalists, educators, judges, civil servants, protesters, Democrats, and independent institutions can all be cast as threats in the public imagination.

That is not only ugly speech. It is a way to sway voters, excuse cruelty, and make suppression seem justified. If a leader can make people believe the real danger is the opponent, then harshness starts to look like protection.

This matters because hate can spread across the conflict. People who oppose cruelty may begin to feel hatred toward those who use it as a weapon. That feeling may be understandable. But the larger system still benefits when everyone becomes easier to frighten, enrage, and divide.

This is not an argument for softness. It is an argument for discipline. We can name cruelty, corruption, authoritarian behavior, and abuse of power without letting hate dictate our methods.

Public opinion also matters here. Many people are not imagining the harm alone. Polls in 2025 and 2026 showed a majority disapproval of several major Trump administration actions and policies, including tariffs, government functioning, parts of immigration enforcement, the economy, and foreign policy. Pew's 2026 international survey also found very low confidence in President Trump's handling of world affairs and worsening views of the United States in many countries.

Numbers do not rescue the nervous system. They do not prevent further harm. But they can remind a reader of something important:

You are not alone in seeing this.

Moral Clarity Is Not the Problem

You do not need to make the harm sound smaller.

You can say:

- This is cruel.
- This is corrupt.

- This is dangerous.
- This is authoritarian.
- This is harming people.
- This is an abuse of power.
- This should be stopped through lawful, organized, democratic action.

None of that requires you to pretend.

None of that requires you to be neutral.

None of that requires you to forgive people who are still doing harm.

Hate adds something else.

Hate says:

I want them erased.

That sentence may cross your mind. It may linger for a while. If it does, do not begin by shaming yourself. Shame only adds another weight to an already heavy load.

Begin by translating it.

Often, underneath hate, there are cleaner wishes:

- I want the harm to stop.
- I want people protected.
- I want accountability.
- I want power removed from those abusing it.
- I want the systems enabling this to fail.
- I want truth to matter again.
- I want a future where cruelty is not rewarded.

Those wishes can become action.

Hate usually cannot.

The Daily Harm Pattern

One reason this is so hard is that the harm does not arrive as a single event. It arrives as a pattern. Something new seems to happen every day, and the body does not get to finish processing yesterday before today brings another threat.

That creates an unfinished alarm. You may wake already braced. You may check the news before your feet hit the floor. You may feel heavy before you know what happened.

You may find yourself asking:

What now?

Who now?

How much worse now?

That is not a weakness. It is what happens when the mind keeps trying to track danger that does not pause long enough to be understood. This is why the answer cannot be simple calm. The answer must include protection, information boundaries, shared action, and recovery.

Shift From Person to Pattern

The person matters. Power held by a person matters. Character matters when it directs public power. But if hate keeps your attention fixed on one face, it can shrink your map.

Action needs a wider map.

Ask:

- What harm is being done?
- Who is being harmed?
- What system is enabling it?
- Who benefits from it?
- Who is already resisting it?
- What lever exists near me?
- What is too large or too risky for me to carry alone?

This does not excuse the person. It helps you stop making him the center of your inner life. You are not here to become a monument to your hatred. You are here to protect life, truth, dignity, community, and the future.

What Action Means When You Cannot Stop It Today

Sometimes people say, "Take action," as if that alone solves the problem. But what if the action you most want is not available today? What if you cannot stop the President, the administration, the court, the agency, the law, the policy, the company, the media machine, or the movement today?

Then action needs a more honest meaning.

Action is any life-serving move that does at least one of these:

- Reduces harm.
- Protects someone reachable.
- Builds future power.
- Preserves truth.
- Strengthens connection.
- Keeps you usable for the long struggle.

This is not pretending that small actions are the same as stopping the whole harm. They are not. But small does not mean meaningless.

One person helped is one person helped. One lie corrected for the right audience is one piece of truth safeguarded. One voter registered is one future lever strengthened. One exhausted body rested is one more person still available tomorrow.

One group of decent people staying connected is one piece of culture that has not been surrendered. You may not control the central harm today. That does not mean you do not matter. It means we need a more honest map of influence.

The Nearest Honest Lever

When helplessness says nothing matters, ask a different question.

Do not ask:

Can I fix this today?

Ask:

Where is the nearest honest lever located?

A lever may be close.

- My body.
- My attention.
- My household.
- My friend who is scared.
- My local community.

A lever may be shared.

- A group already doing good work.
- A call campaign.
- A meeting.
- A protest with a clear purpose.
- A mutual aid network.

A lever may be delayed.

- Voter registration.
- Candidate support.
- Local organizing.
- Court watching.
- Records that may matter later.

A lever may be cultural.

- Refusing cruel language.
- Teaching children what decency means. Keeping art, music, worship, friendship, and hospitality alive.
- Building places where people remember how humans should treat each other.

Choose one lever, not ten. One honest lever is enough for now. Then decide whether today calls for action, preparation, connection, or recovery.

Stop Feeding the Loop

If hate and helplessness are feeding each other, information needs a boundary.

Before you open news or social media, ask:

- What am I trying to learn?

- What decision could this change?
- What action might follow?
- How long will I stay?
- What will I do after I stop?

If you cannot answer, you may not be gathering information. You may be feeding the loop instead.

Try the output rule.

Every heavy news session needs one output.

Examples:

- Save one useful fact.
- Share one accurate item with one person who needs it.
- Make one call.
- Send one donation.
- Add one deadline to the calendar.
- Write one note.
- Choose one recovery action.

The goal is not to turn every headline into a task. The goal is to stop giving attention away without any return.

A Short Practice: Translate The Hate

When hate is loud, write four lines.

First:

The harm I am seeing is:

Second:

The people, places, rights, or future I want protected are:

Third:

The nearest honest lever I can touch is:

Fourth:

My next faithful step is:

The step can be small. It can be a call, a donation, a check-in, or joining work already underway. It can also be closing the feed and sleeping because tomorrow needs you.

The size of the step does not have to match the size of the hate. It only has to remain true to the value beneath it.

Before You Move On

Ask yourself:

- Am I feeding hate?
- Am I using energy?
- Am I recovering capacity?

Feeding hate sounds like:

- I need one more terrible thing.
- I want to see people agree with my hatred. I am looking for proof that they are even worse than I am.
- I am too exhausted to act, yet I cannot stop watching.

Using energy sounds like:

- I know what matters here.
- I am choosing one lever.
- I am acting with others when I can.
- I am protecting someone who is reachable.

Recovering capacity sounds like:

- I am putting the phone down.
- I am moving my body.
- I am going to bed.
- I am making music.
- I am calling someone who brings me back to myself.

All three states are human, but only two help you stay strong. You do not have to love the person who is causing harm. You do not have to forgive what is still happening. You do not have to pretend the harm is smaller than it is.

But you do need to protect your own soul from becoming occupied territory. Keep the harm in view, keep those being harmed closer to the center, and keep one honest lever within reach.

Chapter Five: Why You May Need Additional Coping Strategies

Sometimes an old coping tool stops working, and we take it personally. We assume we have lost discipline or that something in us has broken. Often, the simpler truth is that a good tool has met a job it was never meant to do.

I am not asking you to throw away what has helped you. I want us to sort it out honestly. Which tools still give you strength? Which need more support? What does this situation require that your old approach could not provide?

How To Use This Chapter

Use this chapter when familiar ways of coping no longer work. We will look at whether you need to settle your body, reduce a demand, restore a resource, recruit help, change a circumstance, take action, or rest. If the risk is immediate, use current outside help along with what this book offers.

Why Old Tools Stop Working

Lisa had handled stress well for years. When work overwhelmed her, she took a yoga class. When family troubles arose, she went for long walks. When the news became too heavy, she stepped away from the screen and found her garden or a good book.

Those practices had carried her through a divorce, a difficult boss, her mother's illness, and the everyday chaos of raising two children. Then they were no longer enough.

A weekend away from screens left her facing three new crises on Monday. During meditation, her mind kept returning to threats to her daughter's health care. Gratitude journaling felt hollow because the danger she feared was real.

"I feel broken," she told her therapist.

"Everything that used to help no longer works. I cannot calm down or find my footing." Her therapist had heard the same fear from other clients. "You are not broken," she told Lisa. "The strain has changed, but your tools have not kept pace."

You Are Not Broken

If your usual ways of handling stress have lost some of their effectiveness, you are not alone. Many people who coped well for years are finding that familiar methods cannot withstand a prolonged and uncertain threat.

That does not make the practices useless, nor does it make you a failure. It means we need to understand the job before choosing the tool.

The Difference Between Stress and Ongoing Threat

Most stress advice is framed as a problem with a beginning and an end. You prepare for a presentation, use breathing to settle yourself, give the presentation, and recover. After an argument, you take a walk, return, and work toward a resolution.

These methods help the nervous system return to baseline after a temporary disruption. They can work well when the disruption passes.

An ongoing threat is different. It may be woven into political decisions, public systems, work, health care, or the safety of the people you love. It offers no reliable moment when the body can declare the danger over.

A breathing exercise can lower your immediate alarm, but it cannot repair a public institution. A weekend retreat can restore some capacity, but it cannot resolve a danger that is still unfolding. The practice may be working even as the larger problem remains.

Changing a thought can help when the thought is distorted or when panic has narrowed your perspective. It becomes harmful when we use it to deny an accurate reading of danger.

When democracy is under attack, "Everything happens for a reason" may offer comfort, but it is not a plan and can disconnect us from what the moment demands of us.

Understanding This Through the Coherence Lens

Antonovsky's framework offers a useful way to sort this out. Coherence depends on comprehensibility, manageability, and meaningfulness.

Conventional coping advice often focuses on manageability. It helps calm the body, steady emotions, and restore a sense of control. That work matters, but it is only one part of what people need.

A calming technique cannot, by itself, explain what is happening or connect your response to a larger purpose. When demands exceed your current resources, asking the technique to do all three jobs can leave you ashamed and frightened.

You breathe and stay upset. You meditate, and the danger remains. It is easy to conclude you are doing it wrong when the real problem is a mismatch between the tool and the demand.

Manageability does not mean feeling calm all the time. It means believing that adequate resources are available for the challenges you face.

Some of those resources live within us, but many do not. We depend on other people, community networks, institutions, money, information, transportation, and practical help. A threat that requires a shared response cannot be borne by private coping alone.

When "Self-Care" Becomes Part of the Problem

You may have been told to practice more self-care: sleep, exercise, eat better, take a bath, keep a gratitude journal, or focus on what you can control. Several of these practices help me, and I am not dismissing them.

The trouble begins when self-care is offered as the answer to an organized attack on a person's well-being. Advice meant as support begins to sound like blame.

We need the baseline practices, accurate information, other people, and a strategy. Telling someone whose house is on fire to manage stress better misses the fire.

The hidden message is painful: if you are struggling, you must not be taking care of yourself. That reframes public harm as a private wellness problem and leaves the harmed person responsible for both the injury and the response.

Self-care remains part of staying strong. It restores the capacity we need for judgment, connection, and action. It cannot replace them.

Care, strategy, solidarity, and collective power belong together.

The Limits of Individual Solutions

Much coping advice focuses on an individual's response to a personal problem. But human beings are not built to feel fine while their communities are threatened. Our well-being depends partly on relationships, institutions, culture, and the physical world around us. Distress can be an appropriate response to damage to any of them.

We cannot meditate a democracy back into health or think positively enough to restore another person's rights. Individual practices can steady us for the work, but they cannot do the work in our place.

Antonovsky understood that people draw strength from both personal and shared resources. Emotional skills matter. So do relationships, cultural stability, institutional support, and economic security. When those foundations weaken, individual coping has to carry more than it can reasonably bear.

Why Just "Thinking Positive" Fails Right Now

Positive thinking can help when fear has convinced us that a single bad outcome is the only possible one. It fails when it treats every painful thought as an error.

Concern about democracy may reflect pattern recognition rather than pessimism. Anger at cruelty may reflect moral clarity rather than negativity. If we force a cheerful interpretation onto genuine harm, we lose information we may need.

I have watched violent death replayed on television and social media. I could not make it harmless by choosing a brighter thought. I had to admit what it did to me, including the grief.

Frankl found meaning through an honest encounter with suffering, not by pretending the camps were less horrible than they were. That distinction is important here.

Despair is not our only alternative to forced optimism. We can face what is true, listen to the information in our feelings, and still seek a useful response.

The Problem with "Just Unplug"

Advice to "unplug" can be helpful when repeated exposure is harming us without adding useful information. For some readers, however, staying informed is part of staying safe.

An immigrant may need to track policy changes. An LGBTQ+ person may need to know about new laws. Health care restrictions, enforcement actions, school decisions, and local events can affect what a person must do next. Information is not merely content when it helps protect a life.

The answer is not constant exposure. It is a way to gather what you need without surrendering your nervous system to the feed. We will build that practice in Chapter Seven.

Why Distraction Is not Enough

Distraction has a legitimate place. A funny program, a light book, music, a hobby, or time outdoors can provide the body and mind with needed relief.

The problem arises when relief becomes our only response to an ongoing threat. Avoidance takes energy, the danger persists while we look away, and we may miss information or a chance to prepare.

Use distraction as rest, not as a complete strategy. Let it help you return with greater capacity for the life in front of you.

What You Really Need

When an old coping strategy no longer works, start with a better question: What does this moment require?

You may need to lower the alarm in your body, remove one demand, eat, sleep, obtain medicine or transportation, ask another person for help, change the environment, take action, or allow yourself to rest.

Different moments require different tools. The coherence lens helps us identify where the need lies.

Comprehensibility helps you understand what is happening, recognize patterns, and distinguish useful information from noise.

Manageability helps you identify real resources: personal skills, practical support, trustworthy relationships, and shared capacity.

Meaningfulness connects effort to what you care about, so action is more than frantic motion and rest is more than mere withdrawal.

None of these resources needs to be private. Strength often begins when we stop assuming we must carry the whole load alone.

Honoring Your Distress

Your distress deserves respect. It may be telling the truth about circumstances that would strain any human system.

I will not try to talk you out of what you know, nor will I ask you to pretend the danger is smaller. I do want to help you keep the danger from taking possession of your attention, relationships, health, and purpose.

The practices ahead will help you settle when you are flooded, understand what is happening, build resources, and turn feelings into chosen action. Your older practices may remain part of that work. They do not have to do all of it.

What Comes Next

Chapter Six begins with immediate physiological tools for moments when alarm has pushed clear thinking out of reach. These are first aid, not a complete answer.

Later chapters help you sort information, build practical and social resources, recover meaning, and choose sustainable action. Clarity and strength do not remain private. What steadies you may help you steady someone else.

The aim is to protect what you love without losing yourself along the way.

Before You Move On

Before moving on, spend a few minutes reflecting on three questions. You may write your answers or simply sit with them.

1. Which of your usual coping strategies still helps, even partially? Which no longer helps? A practice that carried you through a difficult boss or a family crisis may have reached its limits. That is information, not failure.
2. How coherent does your world feel today? Rate comprehensibility, manageability, and meaningfulness on a scale of one to ten. The lowest number may indicate where support is most needed.
3. Who seems to be carrying a similar strain with some steadiness? Notice which resources, relationships, limits, or habits may be helping that person. This is observation, not comparison.

If you are highly activated now, Chapter Six is the right place to begin.

Chapter Six: Regaining Your Physiological Footing

When pressure gets high enough, the body is often the first doorway back. That does not mean the whole problem is inside your body. It means your body may be the place where enough capacity returns, allowing you to think, choose, speak, leave, call, rest, or act.

This chapter is a first step, not the whole answer. Use it the way a coach would use a timeout: not to deny the game, but to help you come back with enough steadiness to make the next play.

How To Use This Chapter

Use this chapter when your body or mind is flooded and thinking is hard. You may be panicking, frozen, enraged, numb, scattered, or unable to decide. These body tools are meant to provide first help. They aim to restore enough capacity for the next safer choice. If you are in immediate danger, use safety support first. Body tools can help you act more clearly, but they do not replace protection.

Body Tools For the First Few Minutes

Body tools are for the first few minutes when you are flooded. Use them when you are panicking, frozen, enraged, scattered, numb, or trying to think while your body has taken over. Their purpose is to regain enough capacity for one safer choice, not to solve your whole life.

Start with one tool. Do not read the entire chapter before you begin. Under high stress, one practiced move is better than ten options you cannot use.

Check Safety First

Before using a body tool, check whether this is a safety moment. A calming practice is not the right first step if someone is in immediate danger or if you fear you may harm yourself or someone else.

Ask:

- Am I in immediate danger?
- Is someone else in immediate danger? Am I afraid I might harm myself or someone else?
- Do I need another person with me?

If yes, make safety the first priority. Use trusted people and appropriate local help. Body tools can help you act more clearly. They do not make danger disappear.

Use One Tool Before You Read Everything

When your system is flooded, too many choices can become another burden. This is why the first instruction is simple: use one tool before you read everything.

If you can only do one thing, do this:

- Take a small inhale.
- Take a second small inhale before you exhale.
- Let the exhale be long and slow.
- Look around and name one thing you can see.
- Say, "I am here."

That is enough to start. You can read the rest after your body has a little more room.

Terrence's Alarm System

Terrence was a contractor who prided himself on being practical. If something needed fixing, he fixed it. If something needed figuring out, he figured it out. That approach had served him well for forty years. Then he started waking at three in the morning, his heart pounding. He tried to fix it.

He took sleep supplements. He cut back on coffee. He started going to bed an hour earlier. None of it helped. His wife, Denise, watched him get up night after night, sit at the kitchen table in the dark, and stare at the wall. He was not a man who talked about feelings. Even he admitted that something was wrong.

"My body is acting like there is a fire drill going off every few hours," he told his doctor. "But there is no fire."

His doctor nodded. "There is a fire," she said. "You just cannot see it."

She explained what was happening. Terrence's nervous system had absorbed months of sustained alarm over his community, the country, and the world.

His body did not distinguish between a threat he could physically respond to and a threat that lived in a news feed.

His alarm system had done its job. Now it could not be stood down.

"You have not broken," she said. "Your alarm system has been running overtime. We need to teach it to reduce the alert."

That conversation changed how Terrence understood what was happening to him. He stopped trying to force sleep. He started working with his nervous system instead of against it. It took several weeks. Gradually, the three-o'clock wake-ups stopped.

A Different Way to Think About This

A common cultural approach to stress assumes something unrealistic. It suggests that you should be able to think clearly no matter what is going on around you. If you are overwhelmed, the usual advice is straightforward:

- Try harder.
- Push through.
- Stay focused.
- Get control of yourself.

That model does not align with how human beings work. When threats keep coming, whether physical, emotional, or informational, your nervous system shifts into protection mode.

Your attention narrows. Your body tenses. Your thinking grows less flexible. This is not a personal failure. It is your biology trying to protect you.

The goal of this chapter is not to make you feel perfectly calm in the middle of difficult times.

The goal is more practical:

Help your body settle enough that your thinking can come back online when you need it.

Know Which Phase You Are In

Your capacity changes under stress. That does not mean you are failing. It means the tool has to match your state.

Before choosing a practice, ask which phase best describes you right now. Are you in crisis, where thinking is mostly offline? Are you stabilizing, where a few simple steps are possible? Or are you building, where you can plan for the next time?

There are three broad phases:

- Crisis.
- Stabilizing.
- Building.

Crisis Phase

Use this when your thinking feels mostly offline.

You may notice:

- Trouble focusing.
- Trouble deciding.
- A strong sense of urgency.
- Emotional flooding.
- Freezing or shutting down.
- A need to do something right now, even if you do not know what to do.

In this phase, complex strategies do not work well. Your job is not to understand everything. It is to get a little more oriented.

Use:

- Slow exhale.

- Find the room.
- One safe movement.
- One safe person, if needed.

Stabilizing Phase

Use this when your thoughts return in short bursts.

You may notice:

- You can focus for a few minutes.
- Some decisions feel possible.
- Overwhelm comes and goes.
- You can name one next step.
- You can read a short list, but not a long explanation.

In this phase, simple organizing tools start to help. Your job is to keep the next step small.

Use:

- Name the feeling.
- Four-Box Reset.
- One next action.
- A short text to one safe person.

Building Phase

Use this when you can think more clearly.

You may notice:

- You can plan ahead.
- You can sort several tasks.
- You can choose what matters most.
- You can return to a routine.
- You can prepare for the next time you are flooded.

In this phase, you can build a sequence you can use again.

Use:

- A daily practice.
- A support map.
- A sustainable lane.
- A plan for the next flood.

Crisis Phase Tools

When your system is fully activated, the fastest way back is usually through the body. These tools require very little thought. Use them when you feel hijacked, flooded, or unable to make sense of the situation.

Pick one tool and use it for a minute or two. If it helps, continue. If it does not help, try another tool or reach out to someone. The goal is not to perform the practice well. The goal is to create enough steadiness for the next choice.

Slow Exhale

Use the slow exhale when your body is activated and you need a simple way to lower the alarm. This is often helpful before a difficult conversation, after a news shock, during panic, or when anger is rising too quickly.

- Inhale gently through your nose or mouth.
- Exhale a little longer than you inhale.
- Let your shoulders drop if they will.
- Repeat two or three times.
- Look around and name one thing you can see.

You are not trying to force calm. You are giving your body one small signal that the alert can come down. If the breathing makes you uncomfortable, stop and use a different tool.

STOP

Use STOP when you are close to reacting automatically. It is useful before sending a message, entering an argument, making a decision from panic, or acting while flooded. The purpose is to create a little room between the first impulse and the next choice.

- Stop. Pause whatever you are doing if it is safe to do so.Take a breath. Let the exhale be longer than the inhale.
- Observe. Notice your body, the feeling, the thought, and the room around you.

- Proceed. Choose the next small step rather than letting the impulse choose for you.

Even a brief pause can help the thinking brain re-engage. If the situation is unsafe, do not remain in place just to complete the exercise. Use the pause to move toward safety or support.

Physiological Sigh

Use the physiological sigh when your body feels highly activated and ordinary breathing is hard to settle into. The purpose is to help the body release some built-up tension without needing a long practice.

- Inhale through your nose or mouth.
- Before exhaling, take a second small breath of air.
- Exhale slowly through your mouth.
- Let the next breath be natural.

Try two or three cycles if that helps.Stop if it feels uncomfortable, dizzying, or irritating. No tool works for every body. You can use slow exhale, finding the room, movement, or another steady person instead.

5-4-3-2-1 Grounding

Use this when your mind is racing ahead, your body feels distant, or you feel trapped in a thought or image. The purpose is to bring your attention back to the present moment through your senses.

Notice, slowly:

- 5 things you can see.
- 4 things you can touch.
- 3 things you can hear.
- 2 things you can smell.
- 1 thing you can taste.

You do not have to do it perfectly. If one sense is unavailable, skip it and use another. You are reminding your nervous system that you are here, in this moment, with a body and a place.

Butterfly Hug

Some people find bilateral tapping calming. The butterfly hug is a gentle way to try it. Use it when your body feels stirred up and you want a quiet rhythm that does not require much thought.

- Cross your arms over your chest.
- Rest each hand near the opposite shoulder or upper arm.
- Tap gently, right, left, right, left.
- Continue for one to two minutes if it helps.

When you are finished, let your eyes look around the room. If it feels uncomfortable, irritating, or too emotionally intense, stop. Choose a different tool or reach out to another person. The point is steadiness, not completing a technique.

Putting It Together

Start by identifying your phase. If you are in the Crisis Phase, do not try to solve the whole problem. Use one body tool first. If you are stabilizing, choose one next step. If you are building, make a short plan for the next time your system floods.

The principle is simple:

Match your tools to your current capacity, not to where you wish you were or where someone else thinks you should be, but to where you are right now. That is not giving up. That is how you begin again.

Before You Move On

The tools in this chapter work best when practiced before you need them.

Under high stress, the brain reaches for familiar patterns. An unfamiliar technique may not be available when your system is flooded.

This week, choose one technique:

Slow exhale.

Physiological sigh.

5-4-3-2-1 grounding.

Butterfly Hug.

Practice it once today, when you are not in crisis.

Then identify which phase you are in right now.

- Crisis.
- Stabilizing.
- Building.

Finally, build a short settling sequence. Use two or three steps in order.

For example:

- Step outside.
- Take three slow exhales.
- Text a trusted person.

The sequence signals to your nervous system that the alert can come down.

Your body is not your enemy. It has been trying to protect you.

Now you are learning to work with it.

The next chapter turns to one of the biggest reasons people keep getting reactivated: the constant flood of incoming information.

Chapter Seven: Managing The Information Flood

Information can be a source of care. It can help you protect yourself and the people you love, vote wisely, prepare, and act. Information can also become a delivery system for alarm. The difference is not always the topic. Sometimes the difference is whether the information leads to clarity or only keeps the body activated.

This chapter will not ask you to stop knowing what is happening. It will help you keep information related to safety, action, preparation, connection, or release.

Viewed through the lens of coherence, the information flood is not a side issue. It can hit all three questions at once. If too much is false, too fast, or framed to inflame you, it becomes harder to answer: What is happening? If every source feels suspect, it becomes harder to answer: What can I do? If people are mocked, blamed, or treated as disposable, it becomes harder to answer: What still matters?

This chapter offers one pathway back. It helps you protect your attention so you can regain enough clarity, trust your better judgment, and keep information connected to useful action.

How To Use This Chapter

Use this chapter when news, alerts, posts, rumors, or updates are taking over your attention. The purpose is not to stop knowing what is happening. It is to keep information focused on safety, preparation, action, connection, or release. If you need information for real safety, do not cut yourself off from it. Slow down, choose reliable sources, and get help sorting out what applies to you.

When Staying Informed Starts Hurting

Marcus used to check the news twice a day, morning and evening. A few articles. A short broadcast. Enough to stay reasonably informed. But over the past year, something changed. Now he checks constantly. Notifications trigger a spike in tension. One article turns into twenty open tabs. He goes to bed uneasy and wakes up reaching for his phone. "I know I should stop," he told his wife. "But what if I miss something important?" If this sounds familiar, you are not alone.

Many thoughtful, responsible people have been drawn into the same pattern.

The Real Cost of Information Overload

We often assume that more information leads to better decisions. Past a certain point, the opposite happens. When your system is flooded, more input can make reality feel less clear, not more.

You may notice:

- Everything feels urgent.
- Patterns become harder to see.
- Focus fragments.
- Emotional activation rises.

Instead of feeling informed, you feel scattered and tense. This is not simply a personal discipline issue. Many modern media environments reward whatever captures and holds attention. Recognizing that design helps you stop blaming yourself for what the flood is doing to your mind.

Understanding How You are Being Hooked

Your brain is naturally tuned to notice threats.

Historically, this helped humans survive. Today, that same sensitivity is often used to keep you engaged. Content that reliably captures attention often includes:

- fear cues
- outrage triggers
- artificial urgency
- conflict framing

Over time, repeated exposure keeps your alert system partially active, even when you are safely at home. Recognizing this pattern is the first step toward protecting your attention.

Common Manipulation Patterns to Watch For

You do not need to analyze every article, post, or speech in depth. A tired reader should not have to become a full-time media scholar to stay sane. But it helps to recognize a few common patterns so you can pause before the pattern takes your attention.

Use the next three labels as warning lights. When one appears, slow down and ask whether the information helps you understand, prepare, connect, act, or recover.

Firehosing

Firehosing is a rapid flood of claims, outrage, accusations, and distractions. The point is often not to prove a single thing. The point is to exhaust people so they stop sorting carefully.

When you notice this pattern, slow down. Ask which claim matters, who is making it, what evidence supports it, and whether anything you learned changes a real decision. You do not have to chase every stream in the flood.

Whataboutism

Whataboutism deflects from the issue in front of you by pointing elsewhere. Sometimes the other issue is real. The problem is that the move prevents anyone from answering the first question.

When this happens, return to the original issue. Ask, "What still needs to be answered here?" You can care about more than one harm without letting one harm erase another. If another issue deserves attention, give it its own honest conversation rather than letting it serve as a doorway out of accountability.

False Equivalence

False equivalence presents two situations as if they are the same when they are not comparable in scale, power, intent, or effect. This can cloud judgment and make moral clarity seem unreasonable.

When you notice it, compare the concrete facts. Who has power? Who is being harmed? What was done? What pattern does it belong to? Careful comparison helps you stay fair without pretending unequal things are the same.

Creating a Sustainable Information Diet

An information diet is not about ignorance. It is about choosing how information enters your day so it serves clarity rather than constant alarm. Use this when checking the news leaves you no wiser, only more tense.

Start with one small change:

- Choose one or two reliable sources to check first.
- Set one or two planned times for updates.
- Turn off one notification stream that mostly spikes alarm.
- Avoid late-night scrolling when your body needs to stand down.
- After a thorough check, choose one output: act, prepare, connect, park, or recover.

Notice what changes in your body and thinking. If you are directly at risk, do not cut off access to safety information. Instead, ask a trusted person to help you track what matters or set up a safer way to check for updates.

Before You Open The Feed

If hate and helplessness are feeding each other, do not start by promising to stop caring.

Begin with a boundary.

Before you open news or social media, ask:

- What am I trying to learn?
- What decision could this change?
- What action might follow?
- How long will I stay?
- What will I do after I stop?

If you cannot answer, you may not be gathering information.

You may be feeding the loop.

Try the output rule.

Every heavy news session needs one output.

Examples:

- Save one useful fact.
- Share one accurate item with one person who needs it.
- Make one call.
- Send one donation.
- Add one deadline to the calendar.
- Write one note.
- Choose one recovery action.

The goal is not to turn every headline into a task.

The goal is to stop giving attention away with no return.

The Four-Box Reset

When information overload has already built up, a simple sorting method can help.

The old question was:

Can I act on this, or do I need to release it? That is useful, but it is not enough. Some information does not require action today, but it still deserves preparation. Some information should not be carried alone. Some information is painful, but does not help you act, prepare, or connect.

Use four boxes:

- Act now.
- Prepare.
- Connect or delegate.
- Park or release.

Box 1: Act Now

Ask:

What did I learn that changes what I should do today? This box is for information that points to a concrete step.

Examples:

- Send the message.
- Make the call.
- Save the file.
- Write down what happened.
- Check one current resource.
- Change the plan because safety has changed. Step away from the feed because nothing more is needed right now.

Act now does not mean fixing everything now. It means taking the next step that belongs to you.

Box 2: Prepare

Ask:

What cannot be solved now but can be readied? This is the category a simpler actionor-release pattern can miss. Some things matter, but they are not ready for action yet. They need preparation.

Examples:

- Gather documents.
- Make copies.
- Choose reliable sources.
- Set a time to check updates.
- Write down questions for a professional. Identify who to call if the situation changes.
- Learn which current resources apply.

Preparation is not panic. It is how you reduce future scrambling.

Box 3: Connect Or Delegate

Ask:

What should not be carried alone? This box is for information that requires another person, group, professional, organization, or community.

Examples:

- Ask someone else to help track updates.
- Ask someone to explain an issue they know better.
- Ask someone to sit with you while you decide.
- Ask someone to help document events.
- Contact a group that understands the risk. Tell one trusted person what you are watching for and why.

Connection is not a consolation prize. It is often the right response. Some information becomes more manageable only when it is no longer private.

Box 4: Park Or Release

Ask:

What is not useful to carry right now? This box is for information that consumes strength without giving you a next step.

Examples:

- Speculation.
- Arguments with strangers.
- Repeating the same story in different words.
- Imagined scenes with no decision attached.
- News you cannot act on tonight.
- Other people's opinions that do not change your next step.
- Problems that matter but are not yours to solve today.

Parking is not pretending. Releasing is not indifference. This box protects your limited attention from being wasted where it cannot help.

A Safety Caution

Do not park what needs safety action. Do not release what needs preparation. Do not carry alone what needs another person. Do not turn everything into urgent action. If you are directly at risk, information may matter more than it would to someone outside the situation. Use current, reliable resources. Ask trusted people for help. Treat safety information differently from an alarm with no action attached.

How To Use The Four Boxes After Checking Information

After reading the news, checking updates, or receiving alarming information, take five minutes to pause.

Write four headings:

1. Act now.
1. Prepare.
1. Connect or delegate.
1. Park or release.

Then ask one question at a time:

- What did I learn that changes what I should do to
- What should I prepare?
- Who can help carry, track, explain, or respond to this?
- What can I set down for now?

Do not sort the whole world.
Sort what is loudest in your mind.
Then choose one next step.

What To Try This Week

You do not need to overhaul your entire information life. Start small.

Try one of these:

- Reduce one notification stream.

Choose one reliable source to check first. Set a defined information window. Use the Four-Box Reset after one news check.

Practice one evening without scrolling after the final planned check.

Notice what changes in your body and in your thinking. The goal is not to become uninformed. The goal is to stay clear enough to act where action is yours.

What Comes Next

You have now been offered two related skills. First, you can help your body settle when it is activated. Second, you can sort information so it does not all become an alarm.

Together, these skills help rebuild coherence:

- I can understand enough.
- This still matters.
- I can do something.

The next chapters build on that. They help you reconnect action with meaning, support, strategy, daily practice, and the long game.

Before You Move On

Ask three questions about what you are taking in.

1. What is actually reaching you? List the sources you touched yesterday. Not the ones you mean to use. The ones you actually opened.
1. Which ones left you steadier, and which left you stirred up? You do not need to quit anything yet. Just notice which is which.
1. What is one change you can hold for a week? Smaller is better. One source you check less often. One time of day you close the feed. One thing you read instead.

Write the answers where you will see them. The goal is not a perfect diet. It is knowing what you are taking in, so the flood does not choose for you.

Chapter Eight: When The Risk Is Concrete

Some chapters in this book help you regain inner steadiness. This chapter has a different purpose. When risk is concrete, the first task is protection. The work is not to talk yourself into feeling safe. The work is to slow down enough to use available help, trusted people, and clear next steps.

Use this chapter with respect for your own situation. A reader facing immigration danger, medical risk, workplace retaliation, family danger, public targeting, or digital exposure does not need vague reassurance. They need steady support for practical care.

How To Use This Chapter

Use this chapter when safety, rights, work, family, medical care, immigration, identity, speech, housing, public benefits, or community may be at risk. The purpose is protection, not vague reassurance. Start by asking whether the danger is immediate. If it is, use trusted people and appropriate local help first. If it is not immediate, this chapter helps you identify the risk, find current resources, involve safe people, and take one clear next step.

When The Risk Is Concrete

This chapter offers emotional support, practical sorting, and current-resource guidance. Use it when the danger is not only a feeling but may affect safety, rights, work, medical care, housing, immigration, identity, family, speech, or community.

If there is immediate danger, use trusted people and appropriate local help first. A book can help you slow down, but it should not be the only help you use when safety is at stake.

Maria And Alex

Maria had lived in the United States for fifteen years. She had built a life here: a small business, a home, and friends who felt like family. Her children were American citizens. They spoke with the accent of the Midwest town where they had grown up. She had always known her immigration status was complicated, but she had felt safe. She followed the rules, paid her taxes, and contributed to her community. Then the rhetoric changed. Then the policies changed.

Now she lay awake at night, wondering how quickly she could gather what her children might need if the situation changed. She stopped moving through ordinary places with ordinary ease. "People keep telling me not to worry so much," she told her closest friend. "But they are not the ones checking every night to make sure the papers are in order." Down the road, Alex was grappling with a different kind of fear.

As a transgender teenager, they had finally felt like they were becoming themselves. They had changed their name, started care that helped them feel alive, and found friends who saw them clearly. Their parents had come around after a difficult year. Life was starting to feel possible. Now, laws and policies were changing around them.

Alex watched other young trans people lose access to the care and safety that had helped them survive. They wondered whether their family would have to move. They wondered whether they would lose the life they had just begun to build. "My friends who are not trans keep saying, 'It will be okay, we will fight this,'" Alex said. "But they get to go home and not think about it. I cannot stop thinking about it because it is my life."

Maria's first step was not solving immigration policy. It was choosing one trusted person to sit with her as she gathered questions and sought current, qualified local help.

Alex's first step was not to answer every fear at once. It was to name one trusted adult, one affirming resource, and one practical question the family needed help answering right now.

This Chapter Is For You

If you are like Maria or Alex, the threat is not abstract. You are not only upset by the news. You are watching something touch your body, family, work, medical care, identity, housing, speech, immigration status, public benefits, or community. You may be an immigrant. You may be LGBTQ+. You may be disabled. You may be a person of color.

You may rely on medical care or public systems that are changing or under threat. You may be a journalist, organizer, educator, public worker, caregiver, student, employee, or community leader. You may be trying to protect someone else. The exact risk will vary. The shared experience is this:

Something real may happen to you or to those you love, and standard coping advice may not be enough. You need steadiness, but you also need timely help. You need emotional support, but you also need accurate information. You need to preserve your humanity, but you may also need to make practical decisions.

Concrete Risk Is Different

Concrete risk is distinct from generalized stress. If your rights, safety, medical care, job, housing, family, legal status, or physical safety may be affected, the goal is not to convince yourself that you are fine. The goal is to become steady enough to assess the next step. Your fear may not be political anxiety. It may be accurate threat detection. That does not mean every fear is the whole truth. It does mean the fear deserves respect.

When people say:

- "You are overreacting."
- "That will not really affect you."
- "Stop thinking about it."
- "Just stay positive."

They may be trying to comfort you. They may also be asking you to ignore information that matters. You do not have to argue with them first. You need to ask better questions.

First, Ask Whether the Danger Is Immediate

Before sorting anything else, ask:

- Is anyone in immediate danger? Am I afraid I might harm myself or someone else?
- Is someone else unable to stay safe?
- Do I need another person with me now?
- Is this a moment for local emergency, medical, legal, or safety support?

If the answer is yes, do not try to resolve it through reflection. Use trusted people and appropriate local help. The three coherence questions can wait. Safety comes first.

Name The Kind Of Risk

If the danger is not immediate, name the type of risk. You do not need perfect language. You need enough clarity to know where to find current help.

Possible categories:

- Physical safety.
- Immigration or legal status.
- Protest, speech, or civil rights.
- Work, school, or public services.
- Medical care or disability support.
- Housing, money, or benefits.
- Digital privacy or device safety.
- Family, caregiving, or custody.
- Harassment, intimidation, or surveillance.
- Community violence or targeted hostility.

Different risks require different help. A trusted friend may help you stay steady. A local advocate may know the system. A qualified professional may know the law, a medical issue, a workplace process, or a safety question. A current resource may tell you what has changed. The category matters because it keeps the next step from becoming vague panic.

Do Not Carry Concrete Risk Alone

Concrete risk becomes more dangerous when it stays private. That does not mean telling everyone. It means choosing carefully.

Ask:

- Who is trustworthy with this information?
- Who understands this type of risk?
- Who can stay calm enough to help me think clearly?
- Who can help me find current resources?
- Who should not know the details right now?

Some people are loving but not helpful in this situation. Some people mean well but minimize risk. Some people may create risk by talking too freely. Choose support based on safety, judgment, and fit. You are not looking for a crowd. You are looking for the next trustworthy person or resource.

Use Current Resources

Some help ages well. Breathing, grounding, naming the feeling, asking for support, and choosing one next step will still matter years from now. Other help changes. Laws, policies, technology, and local resources change. What is safe in one place may not be safe in another.

Before relying on any resource, ask:

- Who made this?
- When was it updated?
- Does it apply where I live?
- Is this general information or guidance for my situation?
- Do I need a local advocate, lawyer, provider, union, organization, or other qualified professional?
- Could following this literally increase my risk?

A current resource is not always perfect, but a current, relevant, reliable source is better than a memory, rumor, an old post, or general advice from someone outside the situation.

Use The Four Boxes Under Concrete Risk

The Four-Box Reset still helps when concrete risks are present, but safety has to stay at the center. Use this when too many risks, tasks, warnings, and fears are competing for attention. The purpose is to separate what needs a step today from what needs preparation, another person, or a temporary place to rest.

Ask one question at a time. If you are unsure whether something belongs in safety action or parking, do not park it alone. Bring in a trusted person, advocate, or qualified professional when available and safe.

Act Now

Act now is the next concrete step for today. It is useful when a real risk needs action, but everything feels tangled. The purpose is not to fix the whole danger in one burst. The purpose is to choose one step that reduces risk or increases support.

Ask:

What needs a concrete step today?

Possible next steps include:

- Contact one trusted person.
- Find a current resource.
- Write down one question.
- Make one appointment or call if needed. Move away from an unsafe conversation or setting.
- Use body tools to think before acting.

Do not turn every fear into action. Acting now means taking one step that belongs to today.

Prepare

Prepare is for something that may matter soon but does not need to be solved right now. This is useful when the future feels threatening and your mind wants to rehearse every possible outcome.

Ask:

What may matter soon but does not need to be solved right now?

Preparation may include:

- Listing the questions you need answered.
- Identifying which kind of help fits the risk. Finding the current resource you will check.
- Noticing what information is missing.
- Asking a trusted person to help you think.

Preparation is not panic. It is reducing future scrambling.

Connect Or Delegate

Connect or delegate applies to anything that should not be handled alone. Concrete risk often requires another person because the stakes are too high to handle alone.

Ask:

What should not be carried alone?

Concrete risk often needs someone else:

- A trusted person.
- A local organization.
- A qualified professional.
- A community group.
- A provider or advocate.
- Someone who can help you track updates.

Connection does not mean giving up agency. It means refusing to make high-stakes decisions alone

Park Or Release

Ask:

What is loud but not useful right now?

You may need to park:

- Speculation.
- Arguments with strangers.
- Repeated opinion pieces.
- Worst-case images with no decision attached.
- Other people's minimization.
- Problems that matter but are not yours to solve today.

Do not park what needs safety action. Do not release what needs preparation. But protect your mind from carrying every possible scenario at once.

Documentation, Only If Safe

Documentation can help. It can also increase risk if someone unsafe might find it.

Before documenting, ask:

- Is it safe to write this down?
- Where would it be stored?
- Who could access it?
- Would keeping this record help me request support or current guidance?
- Do I need to consult a local advocate or a qualified professional first?

If it is safe to make a simple record, keep it simple. Use facts, not guesses.

Possible fields:

- Date.
- Time.
- Place.
- What happened.
- Who was present.
- What records or messages exist.

- Where any copies are stored.

Do not exaggerate. Do not draw conclusions you cannot know.

If documentation could make things worse, pause and find safer guidance first.

Digital Safety, Only With Current Guidance

Digital safety depends on the situation. The safest step for one person may pose a risk for another.

Changing passwords, deleting messages, installing apps, changing settings, or moving files can sometimes alert someone to unsafe activity.

This is especially true if someone else may monitor devices, accounts, location, messages, or browsing activity.

Before making changes, ask:

- What am I trying to protect?
- Who might try to access it?
- What would happen if they did?
- Could a sudden change alert someone unsafe?

Do I need current guidance before making any changes?

Use current digital-safety resources when the issue involves devices, accounts, surveillance, stalking, protest, workplace monitoring, or sensitive communication. The book should not tell you which tool is safest. The safest tool depends on the threat and the person using it.

When Professional Help Is Needed

Some situations require support beyond friends and self-help tools.

Consider current local or professional help if:

- You cannot stay safe.
- You may harm yourself or someone else. Panic, depression, trauma responses, or exhaustion are interfering with your daily functioning.

- The risk involves legal, immigration, employment, medical care, benefits, housing, or custody.
- You are not sure whether a step could make things worse.
- Someone has threatened you, followed you, monitored you, or attempted to control your access to help.

Asking for help is not failure. It is often the responsible next step.

Supporter Guidance: If You Are Supporting Someone

If someone you care about is facing a concrete risk, your job is not to take over. Your job is to become safer to tell the truth to.

What helps:

- Believe they know something about their own risk.
- Ask what kind of help would be useful. Offer specific support rather than vague concern.
- Help find current resources if they want them.

Keep their information private. Follow their lead unless immediate safety requires urgent assistance.

What does not help:

- Empty reassurance.
- Arguing about whether the threat is real. Asking them to educate you while they are under pressure.
- Sharing their situation without permission.
- Giving advice outside your knowledge. Making their fear about your feelings.

Support should reduce the load, not add another person for them to manage. **Your Life Still Belongs To You!**

Concrete risk can shrink your world. It can make every day feel like a cycle of monitoring, preparing, waiting, or defending. But your life is more than the risk. You are still a whole person. You still need food, rest, affection, privacy, humor, music, quiet, beauty, and ordinary moments that remind you you are alive. This is not denial.

It is protection. You are protecting the person who has to make decisions. You are protecting the life the risk is trying to crowd out.

Before You Move On

Do three things.

1. Check immediate danger.

Is there immediate danger?

If so, use trusted people and appropriate local help.

2. Name the kind of risk.

Use one plain phrase.

For example:

- This is about immediate safety.
- This is about rights, work, medical care, or privacy.
- This is about my family or someone I love.
- Choose one next support. Not ten. One.

That might be:

- A trusted person.
- A current local resource or organization.
- A qualified professional.
- A written question you need help with.

You do not have to solve the whole situation today.

You need enough steadiness to take the next right step.

That is coherence under concrete risk:

- I can understand enough.
- This still matters.
- I can do something.

The next chapters turn to meaning: what helps people keep going when the risk does not resolve quickly, and how to practice that meaning in everyday life.

Chapter Nine: The Question That Carries You Through

After the first layers of steadiness return, another question often arises: why keep doing this? That question is not a sign of weakness. It may be the mind asking for fuel rather than another technique.

This chapter is not about forced hope or positive thinking. It is about the kind of meaning that helps people keep showing up even when the outcome is uncertain and the work still matters.

How To Use This Chapter

Use this chapter when the first layers of steadiness have returned, but you are wondering why any of this still matters. The purpose is to reconnect with meaning without forcing hope. If you are flooded, in danger, or too depleted to reflect, begin with first help, safety, or a basic support. Meaning is not a demand to grow from pain. It is a source of fuel for staying answerable to life.

The Engine That Powers Everything Else

Remember Antonovsky's framework from Chapter One? Of the three components of coherence, comprehensibility, manageability, and meaningfulness, he treated meaningfulness as central. It is the motivational engine that powers the other two. Think about it. You can understand a situation perfectly (comprehensibility) and have all the tools to handle it (manageability), but if you do not care, if nothing feels worth the effort, you will not use what you have.

The tools will sit unused because there is no reason to pick them up. But when you have strong meaning and are connected to purposes that matter to you, you'll find ways to make sense of confusing situations because you need to. You'll develop resources you do not currently have because you need them to pursue what matters. Meaningfulness does not just help you cope.

It is what makes you want to cope. It is the answer to "Why bother?" This is why Daniel and Elena were stuck. They understood and were managing, but their sense of meaning had been depleted. They'd lost touch with why any of it mattered.

What Frankl Learned in the Camps

Viktor Frankl wrote about people trying to remain human in concentration camps. Disease, violence, starvation, terror, and chance killed many people. No simple idea can explain who lived and who died.

We need to use his work carefully.

Frankl did not give us a formula for survival. He gave us a witness to meaning in conditions where almost everything else had been taken.

He wrote about the task still ahead. A manuscript to finish. A person to love. A truth to tell. A responsibility that had not ended.

He quoted a line often attributed to Nietzsche: "Those who have a 'why' to live can bear almost any 'how.'"

The "why" did not make the suffering any less painful. It did not make the conditions any less brutal. It did not guarantee rescue. But it could give a person a reason to keep choosing life, dignity, and responsibility for one more day.

That is the part that matters here, not because your situation is comparable to a concentration camp. It is not. But because prolonged difficulty with no clear endpoint asks more than acute-stress tools can provide.

You may need sources of meaning that can carry you through years, not just days.

Three Pathways to Meaning

Frankl identified three pathways through which humans find meaning. Each offers a distinct way to connect with purpose when life feels pointless.

You do not need all three at once. One day you may need to give something to the world. Another day you may need to receive beauty, love, or truth. Another day you may need to decide who you will be as you face what cannot yet be changed.

Creative Meaning: What You Give to the World

The first pathway is creation: bringing something into existence that would not exist without you.

This could be:

- A work of art.
- A business.
- A garden.
- A piece of writing.
- A solution to a problem.
- A meal that brings people together.
- A project that helps others.

Creative meaning comes from contributing something uniquely yours. No one else will create exactly what you do.

In the context of what we are facing, creative meaning might arise from:

- Organizing in your community in ways only you can.
- Writing or speaking about what you witness.
- Creating resources that help others. Building a mutual aid network, support group, or organization.
- Raising children or mentoring young people intentionally.
- Making art that captures this moment or brings beauty amid ugliness.

The question for creative meaning:

What can I bring into existence that matters to me?

Experiential Meaning: What You Receive from the World

The second pathway is through experience: receiving what the world offers.

That may include beauty, love, truth, connection, wonder, and joy.

These experiences do not require you to produce anything. They require you to be open to receiving.

Experiential meaning arises from moments of genuine encounter:

- Another person who truly sees you. Natural beauty that stops you in your tracks.
- Music or art that stirs something deep within you.
- Truth that clarifies what was confusing. Love that reminds you what matters.

In dark times, experiential meaning becomes both more difficult and more important.

It is more difficult because stress narrows our attention and makes us less receptive to beauty and connection. More importantly, these experiences remind us of what we are fighting for. Small moments of joy are not escapism. They are experiences of meaning, reminders that goodness exists, beauty is real, and love is possible. Without these experiences, you forget what you are protecting. The question for experiential meaning: What am I receiving from life that I am grateful for?

Attitudinal Meaning: How You Face What Cannot Be Changed

The third pathway is the one Frankl considered uniquely human: finding meaning in how you confront unavoidable suffering.

Some things can be changed and should be fought for. But some circumstances, at least in the short term, cannot be changed.

You cannot personally reverse the political situation overnight. You cannot undo harm that has already occurred. You cannot protect everyone you care about from every threat.

When you face unavoidable difficulty, you still have a choice:

- With dignity or collapse.
- With courage or surrender.
- With compassion or bitterness.
- With integrity intact or your values abandoned.

Frankl wrote about prisoners who shared their last piece of bread with others who were suffering more. They could not change their circumstances, but they could choose who they would be within them.

That choice itself was meaningful.

Attitudinal meaning does not mean pretending that suffering is good. It means that even in suffering, you can choose responses that reflect your deepest values.

You can model for others what it means to maintain humanity under pressure. You can refuse to become what you are fighting against. The question for attitudinal meaning: Who do I want to be in this situation, regardless of the outcome?

When Meaning Collapses

Sometimes meaning does not just fade. It collapses entirely.

This is the period when nothing feels worth doing, every purpose feels hollow, and you cannot find a single reason to keep going.

This can happen:

- When your efforts repeatedly fail to yield results.
- When the people you trusted turn out to support your harm.
- When the scale of the problem overwhelms any sense that you matter. When you are exhausted beyond your capacity to care.
- When losses accumulate faster than you can grieve.

If you are in this place, first know that this is a normal response to abnormal circumstances. Meaninglessness is not a character flaw or a failure of will. It is what happens when you have been carrying too much for too long. Second: meaning usually does not return through thinking. You cannot reason your way back to caring. Meaning returns through experience, through contact with something that moves you despite yourself.

What to Do When Nothing Feels Meaningful

When nothing feels meaningful, do not start by pressuring yourself to find a grand purpose. Pressure can turn meaning into another thing you are failing at. The first goal is to stay connected to life until meaning has room to return.

Try these steps gently:

- Stop trying to force the feeling. Say, "I do not feel meaning right now, and I do not have to punish myself for it."
- Do one small thing that once mattered. Water a plant. Make food for someone. Step outside. Send one kind message. Let the action create a condition in which meaning may return later.
- Seek an experience, not an achievement.
- Listen to music that has moved you before.
- Sit near beauty.
- Spend time with someone who loves you.
- Let yourself receive something.
- Borrow meaning from others if you cannot find your own. Let one trusted person, community, faith, promise, or memory carry you for a while.
- Keep the time horizon short. Your job today may not be to feel inspired. It may be to keep going until the next bit of meaning returns.

If meaninglessness persists for weeks or if you are having thoughts of self-harm, reach out for professional or crisis support. There is no shame in seeking help to get through.

Before You Move On

If you are in a season when meaning feels thin, let this chapter be enough for now. You have named the question. You have been reminded that meaning cannot be forced by shame. You have seen that meaning can come through what you give, what you receive, and how you face what cannot yet be changed.

The next chapter turns that frame into daily practice. It does not ask you to solve the whole question of purpose. Instead, it helps you touch one source of fuel, one value, and one action that can carry you through the next stretch.

Chapter Ten: Rebuilding Meaning In Daily Life

Meaning does not only live in grand answers. It lives in how a day connects to a value, a person, a promise, a place, or a future. When the world feels too large to repair, daily meaning keeps the next step from becoming empty motion.

This chapter turns the meaning frame into practice. It helps you identify what has been fueling you, name values that endure, and connect ordinary actions to something worth serving.

How To Use This Chapter

Use this chapter when you need meaning to feel more concrete. It is especially useful when you are functioning yet feel hollow, when anger or guilt has become your main fuel, or when small actions seem pointless. Move slowly. Choose one practice, use it, then stop. Meaning grows better through contact than through pressure. If a practice feels too large, make it smaller until it fits into the day you have.

Check Your Fuel

Hard times ask a lot of those who care. Fear may get you moving. Anger may give you energy. Outrage may make you feel awake again.

Those fuels are not wrong. They tell you that something has been violated.

But they are expensive fuels. If you rely on them too long, they begin to burn the person using them.

Ask what is carrying you:

- Am I running on fear?
- Am I running on outrage?
- Am I running on guilt?
- Am I running on duty?

- Am I running on love?
- Am I running on purpose?
- Am I running on belonging?
- Am I running on a promise I still believe in?

Do not shame the answer. Tell the truth, then seek fuel that can sustain human life.

Sustainable Sources vs. Depleting Sources

Not all sources of meaning endure equally well over time. Some burn hot and fast, then leave you emptier than before. Others can carry you for years.

Use this section as a fuel check, not as a moral grade. Fear, anger, and guilt may carry you for a while. The question is whether they are the only fuels you have left. If they are, the next task is not shame. The next task is to reconnect with a source that can keep a human being alive within the work.

Sources That Deplete

- Rage. Anger is appropriate and even necessary. But using rage as a primary fuel keeps your nervous system activated and can burn you up. Use anger as information, not as your main energy source.
- Revenge. The desire to see enemies suffer can be motivating, but it ties your well-being to their downfall and can replace the original values you fought for.
- Proving people wrong can help in short bursts, but it makes your purpose depend on other people's opinions.
- Fear of what will happen if you stop. Fear-based motivation keeps you stuck in threat mode and gives your nervous system little room to rest.
- Guilt and obligation. Doing things only because you should often breeds resentment and exhaustion. Purpose should pull you forward, not just push you from behind.

Sources That Sustain

- Love for specific people, communities, places, traditions, and possibilities reminds you what you are protecting.
- Justice. Not revenge, but a commitment to fairness and to human dignity.
- Legacy. What you build for those who come after you.
- Contribution. The satisfaction of giving what you have to offer.
- Growth. Becoming more of who you aspire to be.
- Connection. Belonging to something larger than yourself, such as a community, movement, tradition, or lineage.
- For those who have it, faith can provide sustenance when earthly sources run dry, offering a connection to the sacred or transcendent.

Sustainable sources tend to connect you with others, with the future, and with values larger than your immediate circumstances. Depleting sources tend to be reactive. They are responses to what has been done to you rather than expressions of what you are moving toward.

Clarifying What You Care About

To build sustainable meaning, you need to know what you value, not what you think you should value, not what others expect you to value, but what genuinely matters to you at the deepest level. This is harder than it sounds. We absorb values from family, culture, and political communities without always examining whether they are truly ours. We say we care about things because it seems right to do so. We lose touch with what truly moves us.

The Anger Test

This practice helps you find values by listening to anger without letting it take charge. Use it when you are unsure what you care about most, but you know which violations make you rise inside.

Ask:

- What news stories, events, or behaviors make me most angry?
- Who is being harmed?
- What value is being violated?
- What would protection look like if my values, rather than revenge, chose the next step?

The things that make you most angry often reveal the values that matter most to you.

If you are furious about family separations at the border, you may deeply value family bonds and human dignity. If corruption enrages you, you may deeply value honesty and fairness. If attacks on trans kids infuriate you, you may deeply value people's right to be themselves. Your anger is information about your values. Listen to it, then let your values guide the means.

The Admiration Test

This practice helps you find values by noticing who moves you in a good direction. Use it when anger has been the loudest teacher and you need another doorway into what matters.

Think of people you genuinely admire. They may be famous, or they may be people in your own life.

Ask:

- What about them do I admire?
- Which qualities move me most?
- Which of those qualities do I want to embody?
- What small act today would move me closer to that way of life?

The qualities you most admire in others often reflect the values you most want to live by. Let admiration teach you what you want to become, not only what you oppose.

The Deathbed Test

This practice helps when daily noise has crowded out deeper priorities. Use it only if it feels grounding. If it feels too heavy today, choose the admiration test or a simpler values question instead.

Imagine yourself near the end of your life, looking back with honesty and with mercy.

Ask:

- What would I regret not doing?
- What would I be proud of?
- What would I wish I had paid more attention to?
- What would I wish I had released earlier?

This test can cut through the loudest demands and point to relationships, contribution, courage, repair, joy, and growth. Write one sentence about what you want to protect now, while there is still time to live it.

Writing Your Values

Based on these tests, try to identify three to five core values. These are the principles that matter most to you, that you want to guide your choices, and that you would want to be remembered for. Some possibilities:

- Justice.
- Compassion.
- Truth.
- Family.
- Freedom.
- Creativity.
- Courage.
- Integrity.
- Connection.
- Service.
- Growth.
- Beauty.
- Faith.
- Community.
- Dignity.
- Love.

Write your values in plain language. Then add one sentence under each value describing what it looks like in daily life.

For example:

- Dignity: I treat people as fully human, especially when power makes that easy to forget.
- Truth: I slow down enough to check what I repeat.
- Family: I protect the people entrusted to me without burdening them with my fear.

Put the list somewhere you will see it. These are your anchors, the things you return to when you have lost your way.

Connecting Daily Actions to a Larger Purpose

Values on paper do not create meaning. Meaning comes from living your values by linking your daily actions to the purposes that matter to you. This is both simpler and harder than it sounds. It is simpler because almost any action can connect to meaning if you see the connection. It is harder because under stress, we lose sight of those connections, and our actions can feel pointless.

The "In Service Of" Practice

This practice helps you reconnect ordinary actions to a larger purpose. Use it when your days feel like a string of chores, obligations, or reactions. It does not change every task. It changes the meaning you can find within each task.

Complete this phrase:

"I am doing this in service of..."

For example:

- I am making this meal to nourish the people I love.
- I am going to work to provide for my family and contribute to my community.
- I am taking this walk in service of my health and my ability to keep showing up. I am having this difficult conversation in service of honesty, which I value. I am resting in service of my ability to continue.

Try it with three actions today. If the phrase feels false, do not force it. Instead, ask, "What would make this action serve something I care about?" Sometimes the answer is to do the task differently. Sometimes the answer is to stop doing a task that no longer serves life.

When Small Actions Feel Pointless

A common obstacle to meaning: "What I can do feels so small compared to the size of the problem. How can my tiny actions matter?" This is the wrong frame. The question is not whether your individual action will solve the problem on its own.

The question is whether you are contributing to a cause you believe in.

Every social movement that ever succeeded was built on countless actions, many of which were invisible.

Rosa Parks' refusal to give up her seat mattered because it built on years of organizing and became part of a sustained boycott.

Someone printing a flyer matters more when others are meeting, calling, planning, showing up, writing letters, and carrying the work forward.

Your small action joins others. You cannot see the whole pattern, but you are part of it.

The meaning is not only in the measurable impact of any individual action. It is in your participation in something larger than yourself.

Meaning Through Modeling

There is another way your actions matter that is easy to overlook: you are modeling for others what is possible.

When you maintain your humanity under pressure, you show others it is possible. When you stay engaged without burning out, you demonstrate sustainable resistance. When you treat people with dignity, even when you are stressed, you remind others of what we are fighting for.

You do not know who's watching. You do not know whose hope you sustain by persevering. You do not know the ripples your example creates.

This is not about performing or being perfect. It is about recognizing that how you live is a contribution in itself. Your way of being in the world affects the people around you, who in turn affect those around them.

You Matter, in Part, Because You Matter to Others

Sometimes the most powerful source of meaning is the simplest one:

You matter because the people around you matter to you.

This is not about being important or accomplished. It is about the web of relationships that gives your life meaning.

Someone needs you. Someone is glad you exist. Someone's life is better because you're in it.

If you are having trouble believing your actions matter in the grand scheme, start small.

Ask:

- Do you matter to your children?
- Your partner?
- Your friends?
- Your coworkers?
- Your neighbors?
- The people you help?

That mattering is real. It is no less important than mattering on a national scale.

For most of human history, people found meaning primarily in their relationships and communities, not in participation in large-scale events.

When you take care of yourself, you are protecting someone who matters to others. When you stay steady, you are a source of stability for those who need it. When you do not give up, you are showing those who look to you that giving up is not required.

You are, in ways you may not fully recognize, someone else's reason to keep going.

Rebuilding Meaningfulness

If your sense of meaning has been depleted, it can be rebuilt. It takes time and usually happens gradually rather than all at once.

Try three small practices:

1. Morning purpose connection, two minutes.

Before you start your day, ask:

- What am I protecting or creating today, And who benefits from my efforts?
- How does today's action align with what I care about?
- Throughout the day.

Practice "in service of" with at least three actions.

Notice when you are contributing to something larger than yourself.

2. Evening reflection, two minutes.

Ask:

- What did I do today that mattered?
- How did my presence affect others?
- What am I grateful for?

Weekly Practices

Weekly practice gives meaning more room than a hard day may allow. Use this when the daily practice has become too small or when you want to notice patterns over several days.

Choose one of these, not all three unless you have the space.

1. Values check-in.

Ask:

- Did I live my values this week? Where did I stay true to them?

What adjustment do I want to make?

2. Meaning inventory.

Ask:

- What gave me energy this week?
- What drained me?
- What felt meaningful?

3. Connection tending.

Ask:

- Who matters to me?
- Have I been in contact with them?
- Who might need to hear from me?

End by choosing one small adjustment for the next week. The point is not to grade yourself. The point is to keep meaning in contact with ordinary life.

When You Need a Deeper Reset

Sometimes the daily and weekly practices are not enough. You need to step back and reconnect with meaning on a deeper level.

Consider:

- A day or a weekend dedicated to reflection, away from the news and obligations. Time in nature, which has a way of restoring perspective.
- Extended conversations with people who know you well and can remind you of who you are.
- Revisiting places, music, books, or experiences that have been meaningful to you.
- Creative projects that express what you have not been able to put into words. Service to others. Sometimes, helping someone else reconnects you with your own purpose.

Finding Their Why

Daniel began with the anger test. What infuriated him most? The cruelty. The casual willingness to harm vulnerable people. He realized that beneath it all, he was driven by a core value: human dignity. Everyone deserved to be treated as fully human, regardless of immigration status, gender identity, race, or political views. Once he named that value, he could begin connecting his daily actions to it. Making breakfast for his kids was not just routine. It was caring for human beings whose dignity he was nurturing.

Going to work was not just an obligation. It was about contributing to a community where people treated each other with respect. Even his self-care was in service of something: staying healthy enough to keep protecting dignity in his small sphere. The tools did not change. What changed was that he now knew what they were for. Elena took a different path. She'd been burning out because her sense of meaning was tied to outcomes, and those outcomes were not coming.

She thought her efforts were meaningful only if they worked. She began shifting toward an attitudinal sense of meaning. She could not control whether the political situation improved, but she could control who she was in the face of it. She decided her meaning would come from refusing to become cynical, from maintaining her capacity for joy and connection even while fighting, and from modeling for her nieces what it meant to stay engaged without being destroyed. She still worked for change.

But her sense of purpose no longer depended on whether change would come in her lifetime. She was participating in something far longer than her own life: a multi-generational project to build a more just world. That reframing made all the difference.

Before You Move On

Meaning does not become real by thinking about it. It becomes real through small, repeated acts of living it.

This week, do three things.

1. Write your why in one sentence.

Not a paragraph. One sentence.

Make it plain enough to read on a hard morning when you have forgotten why any of this matters.

It does not have to be beautiful. It only has to be true.

2. Identify one action from this past week that connected to that why.

It may be small.

A conversation you had. Something you made, protected, or stood up for.

If you cannot find anything, it is worth knowing.

What would one small, purposeful act look like tomorrow?

3. Ask which lineage you belong to.

Which people from history, your community, or your own life were engaged in something similar to what you are trying to do?

You did not invent this. You are continuing something.

Naming that continuity can change how the work feels, especially on days when it seems to lead nowhere.

Meaning does not require certainty of outcomes.

It requires a connection to something worth caring about. You already have that.

The question is whether you are reminding yourself of it often enough.

What is Coming Next?

Meaningfulness becomes stronger when it is not carried alone.

The next chapter explores support and community: how to find the people who help you stay steady, think clearly, act wisely, rest honestly, and remember who you are.

You have turned toward what keeps you going. Now we turn toward the relationships that help sustain that strength.

Chapter Eleven: The Web That Holds You

Few people can stay coherent on their own for very long. You may have inner strength, good tools, and a clear sense of purpose, yet still need other people. That is not a flaw in your resilience. It is part of being human.

This chapter treats community as a real resource, not a decorative extra. The question is not only who loves you but who helps you get steady, think clearly, act wisely, rest honestly, and remember who you are.

How To Use This Chapter

Use this chapter when you are carrying too much alone. It is meant to help you see support as a real resource, not a sign that your private strength has failed. You will map who helps your body settle, who helps you think, who believes in you, who shares your purpose, and who could help in a crisis. Not everyone is safe with every part of your life, so choose support based on fit, trust, and the kind of help needed.

The Web That Holds You

Carmen had been practicing everything in this book for three months. She had the Four-Box Reset down to a T. She could name what she was feeling before letting it drive her. Her information boundaries were solid. She had clarified her values and could connect her daily actions to a larger purpose.

And she was still struggling. She was not falling apart the way she had before. The tools genuinely helped with that. But she felt like she was holding herself together through sheer individual effort, and the effort was exhausting.

Every morning, she had to rebuild her sense of stability from scratch. Every crisis required her to draw on resources entirely from within herself.

"I'm doing all the right things," she told her cousin Miguel. "But I feel like I'm trying to hold up a building by myself. How long can one person keep this up?"

Miguel had been feeling something similar. He had developed strong individual practices, but he had also noticed something else. On the days when he connected with certain people, really connected, not just scrolling past their posts, everything was easier. His nervous system calmed more quickly.

His thinking cleared more quickly, and his sense of meaning felt more solid. "I don't think we're supposed to do this alone," he said. "I think the tools work better when others are involved." He was right. Understanding why changes everything about how you build resilience.

The Resource You Cannot Build Alone

Remember the resistance resources from Chapter One?

Antonovsky identified several types of resources that can help people move toward health under stress.

So far, we have focused mostly on the ones you can develop on your own:

- Cognitive resources, such as understanding.
- Emotional resources, such as regulation. Coping strategies, such as the tools in this book.

But look again at the broader list. At least three categories are inherently relational:

- Interpersonal-relational resources: social support, intimate ties, and connections with others who can offer practical and emotional assistance.
- Macro-sociocultural resources: access to community institutions, cultural connections, and membership in groups larger than yourself.

- Material resources: while partly individual, they are often accessed through relationships. Someone you know may help you find a job, lend you money in an emergency, or share resources during scarcity.

Antonovsky was not merely listing nice-to-haves. Social connection is one of the resources that can make stress more manageable. This is not surprising when you consider it.

Humans are social creatures. We often regulate more easily when connected to others. Our sense of meaning is largely relational. We matter because we matter to others. Our sense-making improves when we can make sense of things together. The tools you have learned are genuinely powerful, but they often work better when you are embedded in a web of supportive relationships.

Your Nervous System Needs Other People

Another steady person can help your system settle. This is not just a pleasant feeling. Your body picks up cues from the people around you. Facial expressions, tone of voice, body posture, and breathing patterns can all influence whether you feel safer or more threatened.

For many people, the presence, voice, or steady attention of a safe person can reduce the effort of calming alone. A calm voice on the phone can help interrupt a spiral. Being near someone who is grounded can help you feel less alone in your fear.

This is also why isolation is so destabilizing. Without safe people to connect with, your system must do more of the work on its own.

That is possible. The individual tools in this book help you do exactly that. But it is harder and more exhausting than it should be.

Community is not a sentimental luxury. It is one of the resources that help people last.

Why Connection Is Hard Right Now

If community is so important, why do so many of us feel isolated? Several forces are working against connection: Political polarization has fractured relationships. People have lost friends, become estranged from family, or learned that neighbors they thought they knew hold views they find abhorrent.

The pool of people who feel safe has shrunk. Trust has eroded. When you are unsure who might report, judge, or turn on you, vulnerability feels dangerous. The openness that fosters connection also exposes you. Everyone is depleted. Building and maintaining relationships takes energy. When everyone is running on empty, there is less capacity for the presence and attention that foster genuine connection.

Geography and mobility scatter people. Your closest friends might live across the country. The people physically near you might not be the ones you'd choose to be near.

Digital connection is not the same. Social media creates an illusion of connection, often leaving people feeling more isolated.

Screens can help us stay in touch. They do not always give the body what in-person presence offers.

These obstacles are real. Building community right now is genuinely difficult.

But it is not impossible. Given how essential it is, it is worth the effort.

What You Are Looking For

When we talk about community as a resource for resistance, we are not talking about popularity, constant contact, or having hundreds of people around you. We are talking about specific kinds of relationships that serve specific functions.

Use these categories to identify what support you already have and what may be missing. One person may fit more than one category. Some people who love you may not fit any category safely right now.

People Who Regulate You

These are people whose presence helps your body settle.

When you are around them, you feel safer. Your breathing may slow, and your vigilance may decrease. You can let your guard down.

You might not even talk about anything important. Just being in their presence helps.

These relationships give your nervous system a break from constant self-regulation. You probably already know these people.

The friend whose voice on the phone instantly makes you feel better.

The family member whose home feels like a refuge. The colleague whose steady presence makes difficult meetings bearable.

People Who Help You Think

These are people who help you make sense of confusing situations. When you talk things through with them, you understand more clearly. They offer perspectives you would not find on your own. They help you see patterns you would otherwise miss.

These relationships build understanding. Two people thinking together can make sense of what neither could understand alone. Your confusion becomes clearer through dialogue. You are not asking them to think for you. You are letting another steady mind help you find the edges of the problem.

People Who Believe in You

These are people who see your capabilities even when you cannot. When you feel helpless, they remind you of what you are capable of. When you want to give up, they express confidence that you can keep going.

These relationships make management easier. Believing in yourself is easier when someone else believes in you first. Their faith becomes something you can borrow until your own faith returns.

People Who Share Your Purpose

These are people who care about what you care about. You are working toward similar goals, fighting for similar values, and trying to create or protect similar things. When you are with them, your efforts feel less solitary. These relationships give your efforts meaning. A shared purpose is more sustainable than an isolated one. When you are part of a group working toward something that matters, your individual contributions feel more significant.

People Who Would Help in a Crisis

These are people you could call at 3 am. People who would show up if you needed them. People who would lend you money, offer you a place to stay, and help you through an emergency. These relationships provide practical security.

Knowing you are not alone if disaster strikes reduces the background anxiety of living in uncertain times. You do not have to handle everything yourself because you have backup.

You do not need dozens of people in each category. A few genuine connections in each area create a web strong enough to hold you up.

The Support Map

Before you can strengthen your community, you need to assess what you already have.

These are not types of people. They are types of support. The same person may fall into more than one category, and some people who love you may not be safe with every part of your life.

Take a few minutes. Write names under five headings.

You do not need to fill out every heading perfectly. Start with the names that come easily.

1. People who help my body settle.

   Ask:

- Whose presence helps me feel more steady?

- Who can I be around without keeping my guard up all the time?

2. People who help me think.

   Ask:

- Who helps me make sense of confusing things?
- Whose perspective helps me see more clearly?

3. People who believe in me.

   Ask:

- Who sees my capabilities?
- Who reminds me of what I can do when I forget it?

4. People who share my purpose.

   Ask:

- Who cares about the same things I do?
- Who is working toward similar goals?

5. People who would help in a crisis.

   Ask:

- Who could I call in an emergency? Who would come?

  Then notice the pattern.

- The same person may appear in multiple categories.
- Some categories may be empty or sparse. Some relationships may have weakened or become complicated.

That tells you where your community-building effort may need to go next.

People you used to count on might now feel unsafe because of political differences. People who used to regulate you might now be so dysregulated that they add to your stress. This assessment is not about judgment. It is about seeing clearly what resources you have right now.

Before You Move On

Pause to review the support map before rushing into building more relationships. The first task is to see what already exists. Some readers will discover more support than they expected. Others will see important gaps. Both discoveries matter.

The next chapter helps you strengthen your web in practical ways: tending to existing relationships, deepening promising ones, finding new people, using vulnerability with care, and building practical support systems.

Chapter Twelve: Building And Protecting Your Web

A support map is only the beginning. Relationships need tending. New trust needs time. Community needs practical care, not just good feelings.

This chapter helps you build and protect the web that makes resilience less lonely. It keeps the work concrete: one relationship, one gap, one offer, one boundary, and one repair.

How To Use This Chapter

Use this chapter after you have identified the support you already have. It is useful when your map feels thin, when old relationships have changed, or when you need practical support that one person cannot provide alone. Start small. Do not make community-building another way to fail. One honest reach toward connection can matter. The point is not to build a perfect circle. The point is to make the next strand of the web a little stronger.

Strengthening Your Web

Once you have mapped your current connections, you can begin strengthening them. This is not about a massive social overhaul. Small, consistent investments in relationships build more resilience than dramatic gestures.

Choose one relationship practice at a time. The goal is to strengthen the web without making connections feel like another performance demand. If you are depleted, the practice may be as small as sending one warm message or accepting one honest offer of help.

Tend Existing Relationships

The relationships you already have are your most valuable resource. They have a history, trust, and mutual understanding that new relationships take years to build.

Tending means regular contact, even when you do not need anything.

Try small practices:

- Send a text to let someone know you are thinking of them.
- Make a phone call just to catch up.
- Show up for the small things, not only the crises.
- Ask how people are doing and listen.
- Offer support when you can.
- Let yourself be a resource to others, not just a recipient.

It also means reciprocity. Relationships where one person always gives and the other always receives eventually become depleted.

Deepen Promising Connections

Use this when your support map shows people who could grow closer if someone took the next small risk. Many friendships stall not because people do not care, but because no one reaches beyond the familiar pattern.

Choose one person who seems promising and reasonably safe. Then take one step:

- Suggest coffee, a walk, a call, or a shared task.
- Ask a question that invites a genuine answer. Share something a little more personal than usual.
- Notice whether they respond with care, curiosity, or reciprocity.

Do not rush intimacy. You are testing for fit and trust over time. If the person does not respond, let that be information, not a verdict on you.

Find Your People

If your map revealed significant gaps, especially in shared purpose, you may need to build new connections.

Start with places where people are already gathering around something you care about.

- Volunteer organizations.
- Community groups.
- Religious or spiritual communities.
- Hobby groups.
- Political organizing.
- Classes or workshops.

The people you meet there already have something in common with you.

Online communities can be a starting point, especially if your identity, concern, or interest is rare in your area.

When possible, move slowly toward an in-person connection.

Your body often interprets physical presence differently than words on a screen.

Be patient. Trust takes time.

You are not seeking instant intimacy. You are looking for people worth investing in over months and years.

The Vulnerability Dilemma

Genuine connection requires vulnerability. You cannot be truly known, and therefore truly supported, if you are always guarded. But vulnerability is especially risky when trust has been damaged or when parts of your life carry real risk.

The question is not whether to open everything or hide everything. It is how to open slowly, wisely, and with attention to safety. The goal is connection that can hold truth, not exposure that leaves you less safe.

Graduated Vulnerability

Graduated vulnerability helps you build connection without handing someone more of your life than they have earned. Use it when you want to be known but are not yet sure whether the other person is safe with the truth.

Start small. Share something real but not devastating. Watch how the person responds. Do they listen? Do they mock, dismiss, gossip, compete, or turn the focus back to themselves? Do they keep the confidence? Do they share something of their own without making you responsible for them?

If the response is careless or harmful, you have learned something at a lower cost. If the response is respectful, you may choose to share a little more later. Trust is built through repeated small tests, not a single dramatic disclosure.

Selective Authenticity

You can be authentic about different things with different people. You might share your political fears with certain friends and your parenting struggles with others. You might be open about your health with family but not with colleagues.

This is not about being fake. It is about being thoughtful about which parts of yourself you share with whom. Not everyone needs access to everything. Safety, trust, and fit matter. **Safe Enough, Not Perfectly Safe**

No relationship is perfectly safe. People disappoint, misunderstand, and sometimes hurt us. Waiting for guaranteed safety means waiting forever. The question is not whether a relationship is risk-free. It is whether the potential benefits justify the risks and whether you can recover if things go wrong. Some vulnerability is necessary for the connection.

The goal is to take reasonable risks, not to eliminate all risk.

Mutual Aid: Practical Support Systems

Mutual aid is practical community care. It is useful when formal systems are strained, slow, absent, or hard to trust. Its purpose is to reduce isolation and make needs more manageable by sharing what people can offer.

Mutual aid can be informal, such as neighbors checking on one another, families sharing childcare, or friends providing rides and meals. It can also be organized through community groups, religious communities, tool libraries, community fridges, or skill shares.

What Mutual Aid Looks Like

Mutual aid can be as simple as neighbors sharing tools, trading childcare, or checking on one another during emergencies. It can also be as organized as community groups coordinating food distribution, providing transportation, or offering legal support. The key distinction from charity is that mutual aid is reciprocal. Everyone both gives and receives, based on what they have and what they need. It is not about helpers and the helped. It is community members supporting each other.

Starting Small

You do not need to create an organization to practice mutual aid.

Start with two questions:

- What can I offer? What do I need?

Then look at your existing network.

Ask:

- Who might be willing to trade support?
- Who already helps in small ways?
- Who might need the kind of help I can offer?

Mutual aid can be informal.

It might look like:

- A few families helping each other with childcare.

- Friends sharing resources when someone is short.
- Neighbors watching out for each other.

  These arrangements may seem small.

  They create real security.

Finding Existing Networks

Mutual aid networks exist in many communities. Search for mutual aid groups in your area. Look for community fridges, tool libraries, buy-nothing groups, time banks, or skill shares. Many religious communities have informal mutual aid embedded in their culture. Joining existing networks is often easier than starting from scratch. You can learn how they work, build trust gradually, and contribute in ways that fit your capacity.

Protecting Your Community

Relationships require maintenance, especially during difficult times. Use this section after you have begun building or naming your web. Its purpose is to keep the web human, reciprocal, and strong enough to withstand ordinary strain.

You do not need a perfect community. You need enough trust, repair, contact, and shared care so people can keep reaching for one another. Three habits matter most, and each can start small this week.

Do not Only Reach Out in Crisis

If you contact people only when you need something, relationships can start to feel transactional. Regular connection during ordinary times builds the trust that sustains relationships through hard times.

Choose one small, non-crisis contact this week. Send a message, make a call, share a meal, ask how someone is, or let them know you were thinking of them. Warmth is easier to find in a crisis when it has been tended before the crisis.

Manage Conflict Constructively

Disagreements are inevitable, especially in stressful times.

How you handle conflict can either strengthen or weaken a relationship.

When conflict appears, try this:

- Address issues before they fester.
- Assume good intent when you can.
- Listen to understand, not merely to respond.
- Apologize when you have caused harm.
- Accept sincere apologies when offered.

Not every relationship can or should withstand every conflict.

But many relationships end unnecessarily because people were never taught how to repair them well.

Accept Imperfection

No one will support you perfectly. People will disappoint you, misunderstand you, and be unavailable when you need them. If you demand perfection, you will end up alone.

The question is not whether someone fails you sometimes. The question is whether the relationship, overall, provides more support than it costs, whether repair is possible, and whether you are better off having this person in your life.

Grieve Lost Connections

Some relationships will not survive this period. Political divisions, shifting values, betrayal, fear, or simply growing in different directions can end connections that once mattered.

Let yourself grieve these losses. They are real, even if the relationship needed to end. Grief is how you honor what was meaningful and, slowly, make room for new connection. You do not have to call the loss small just because the boundary was necessary.

Being a Resource for Others

Community is reciprocal. As you build your web of support, you also become part of others' webs.

This does not mean you must become endlessly available. It means your growing steadiness, knowledge, care, and presence may help someone else hold on. Offer what is real, maintain your limits, and keep contributions human-sized. Support is most trustworthy when it does not require you to disappear.

Offer What You Have

You do not need to be perfectly stable to support others. You can offer whatever capacity you have, even if it is limited. Maybe you can be a stabilizing presence for someone even as you work on your own regulation. Maybe you can help someone think through a problem even as you grapple with your own confusion. Maybe your developing tools can benefit others who are earlier in the process. The goal is not to fix anyone or take responsibility for anyone's well-being. It is to be available in whatever ways you genuinely can.

Model Without Preaching

The most powerful way to help others build resilience is to model it in your own life. When people see you stay grounded amid chaos, they learn that groundedness is possible. When they see you use tools effectively, they become curious about them. You do not need to lecture people about resilience or push them to adopt your practices. Simply living your values visibly is enough. Those who are ready will notice and ask.

Know Your Limits

Supporting others beyond your capacity does not help anyone. It depletes you and may leave you unavailable when you are truly needed.

It is okay to say no. It is okay to set boundaries. It is okay to care for yourself first when you need to. Sustainable community contribution requires sustainable self-care. Setting limits can be one way to keep love from turning into resentment.

A Web That Holds

Carmen started mapping her web and realized she had more than she'd thought, but also significant gaps. She had people who helped her think (her sister and one close friend) and people who would help in a crisis (her parents, despite their political differences).

But she'd lost her support network when her best friend moved away, and she had no one locally who shared her deepest concerns about what was happening in the country. She started small. She reached out to a former colleague she'd always liked but never gotten to know well. She found a local group working on an issue she cared about and began attending. She committed to calling her sister weekly instead of just texting.

Miguel invested in his neighborhood.

He organized a simple text chain for people on his block to check in on one another. He began meeting his elderly neighbor for coffee once a week. He deepened a friendship with someone from his gym who shared his values. Neither built a massive network. But six months later, both reported the same thing: the tools now worked better. Not because the tools had changed, but because people were around to help when the tools were not enough.

They were no longer holding up buildings alone. They were part of structures that held them, too. This is what community does. It does not replace individual work. It amplifies it. It provides backup when your resources run low. It reminds you that you are not alone in caring, not alone in struggling, and not alone in trying to stay strong during difficult times.

What Comes Next

You now have a clearer map of support and a set of practices to strengthen the web around you.

The next chapter turns toward action. Once you are no longer holding everything alone, you can make better choices about where to put your effort.

The question becomes: what is the nearest honest lever, and which lane can you sustain?

Before You Move On

Community does not build itself.

Here are three ways to start this week.

1. Map your web.

Take a sheet of paper and put your name in the center.

Write the names of the people in your life in rings around it. Use the innermost ring for those you trust most deeply, and the outer rings for the rest.

Look at what you have.

Look at where the gaps are.

Most people find the map more populated than they expected. They also notice at least one gap that matters.

2. Close one gap a little.

Reach out to someone whose name appeared in an outer ring.

This may be someone you have been meaning to reconnect with, or someone whose presence in your life has grown passive.

You do not have to ask for anything.

Just close the distance slightly.

A short message, a phone call, or a cup of coffee can be enough.

Relationships do not remain warm on their own.

3. Notice what you already give.

We often think of community in terms of what we receive from it.

But the web holds us partly because we hold it.

Identify one way you are already contributing to someone else's stability.

It may be something you do informally, without naming it.

This is not a small thing.

It is part of what makes you someone others will reach toward when they need to.

Chapter Thirteen: From Reaction To Strategy

Feeling that you matter often returns through action. But action has to be shaped. If every outrage consumes all of you, your strength will scatter. If you do nothing because you cannot do everything, helplessness wins too much ground.

This chapter is about right-sized action. It helps you find one honest lever, choose one sustainable lane, and stop measuring your worth by whether you can stop the harm today.

How To Use This Chapter

Use this chapter when you care deeply but your effort is scattered, reactive, or burning you out. The purpose is right-sized action. You will look for the nearest honest lever, choose a sustainable lane, and stop measuring your worth by whether you can stop the whole harm today. If you need first help, safety support, or recovery before strategy, begin there. Strategy should not become another way to overburden yourself.

From Reaction to Strategy

For the first six months after the election, Keisha was on fire. She attended every protest, signed every petition, called her representatives daily, shared everything on social media, argued with anyone who disagreed, and stayed up late reading about every new outrage.

She was doing something. She was fighting back. Then she crashed. Not gradually. Suddenly. One morning, she could not get out of bed. The thought of another phone call, another march, another argument made her want to cry.

She had gone from feeling she could change the world to feeling that nothing she did mattered.

"I burned myself out," she told her therapist.

"I was running on rage, and the rage ran out. Now I can't do anything at all." Meanwhile, her neighbor James had taken a different approach. He had felt the same urgency Keisha did, but something held him back from trying to do everything at once. Instead, he chose one organization whose work he believed in and committed to showing up consistently.

Two years later, James was still going. His contributions had grown as he learned and built relationships. He had not changed the world, but he had helped change his community in small, concrete ways. "I used to feel guilty for not doing more," James said. "Everyone around me was going to five things a week, but most of them burned out. I'm still here."

This chapter explores the difference between reactive and strategic engagement. It is about becoming more like James than Keisha without losing the fire that makes you care.

The Burnout Trap

Burnout is not a failure. It is the predictable outcome of unsustainable effort.

When something terrible is happening, the natural response is to throw everything you have at stopping it. That feels morally right.

How can you pace yourself when people are suffering? How can you take breaks while the crisis is ongoing?

But the crisis is not a sprint. It is a long race with no clear finish line in sight.

The strategies that feel most urgent and morally compelling in the short term are often exactly the wrong approach for sustained engagement. Reactive engagement responds to every outrage with maximum intensity. It runs on anger, fear, and adrenaline. It measures success by the effort expended, such as how many calls made, how many protests attended, and how exhausted you feel afterward. Strategic engagement focuses on where you can have real impact. It runs on values, purpose, and sustainable commitment.

It measures success by the outcomes achieved, however small, over time. Reactive engagement burns bright and then burns out. Strategic engagement builds power over the years.

Why Anger Is not Enough

Anger matters. It signals that something is wrong, provides initial energy for action, and is an appropriate response to injustice.

But anger is a poor fuel for sustained effort.

Physiologically, anger triggers your stress response. Your heart rate rises, cortisol floods your system, and fight-or-flight kicks in.

This is useful for short bursts of intense action, but it is not built for steady, long-term work.

You cannot stay angry for years without paying a price for your health.

Even if you could, anger distorts judgment and makes you reactive rather than strategic.

It drives you toward whatever feels most satisfying in the moment rather than what is most effective in the long run.

Anger is the spark, not the fuel.

You need something else to keep going after the initial fire dies down.

Remember Chapter Nine? Sustainable sources of meaning include love, justice, legacy, contribution, and connection. These can sustain you for decades, whereas rage burns out in months.

The goal is not to stop being angry; the situation deserves anger. The goal is to channel anger into initial action while building sustainable motivation underneath.

Control, Influence, And Mattering

When the harm is significant, people often ask the wrong question first.

They ask:

Can I stop this?

Most of the time, one person cannot.

If that is the only question, the answer may feel like a no.

Then helplessness takes over.

Use a more honest set of questions.

Control asks:

Can I make this outcome happen on my own?

Influence asks:

Can I make a real difference somewhere in the system?

Mattering asks:

Does my presence, care, action, truth-telling, protection, or endurance matter?

The answer to the first question may be no.

The answer to the third must remain yes.

You matter even when you cannot control the core harm.

Your influence may be close, shared, delayed, protective, cultural, or civic.

That does not make it fake.

It makes it human-sized.

The Nearest Honest Lever

When everything feels too large, ask:

Where is the nearest honest lever located?

Look in several places.

1.Your body and capacity.

Ask:

- What keeps me usable?
- What needs to be protected so I can continue?

2. Your attention.

Ask:

- What information helps me act?
- What information only keeps me activated?

3. Your relationships.

Ask:

- Who needs to hear from me? Who helps me think?
- Who shares my values?

4.Your local world.

Ask:

- What can be protected close to me?
- Which person, group, school, library, clinic, neighborhood, or organization needs support?

5.Your civic power.

Ask:

- What vote, call, meeting, registration effort, testimony, donation, or local campaign can I support?
- Who is already organizing well?

6.Your culture.

Ask:

What humane answer must be kept alive?

What will I refuse to normalize? What can I teach, model, create, host, or protect? Choose one lever.

Then choose the kind of step.

- Act.
- Prepare.
- Connect.
- Recover.

If you cannot act today, you may still be able to prepare.

If you cannot prepare on your own, you may still be able to connect.

If you cannot connect today, you may need to recover so you can connect tomorrow.

None of this means the harm is minor.

It means you are still part of the story.

Choose a Sustainable Lane

You cannot fight everything. Trying to fight everything guarantees you'll be ineffective at everything.

This feels wrong, even when everything feels urgent.

If children are in cages, voting rights are under attack, healthcare is being gutted, the climate is collapsing, and authoritarianism is rising, how could you possibly choose?

You choose because you have to.

Your time, energy, and attention are finite. Spreading them across everything leaves them too thin to matter anywhere.

A lane is not a cage. It is a way to give your care shape.

Your lane can change. It can widen later. It can narrow during hard seasons. It can shift when your health, family, work, or risk changes.

The point is not to limit your care. It is to choose work you can return to.

Criteria for Choosing

Use three filters.

1. Fit

   Ask:

- What skills, resources, and position do I bring?
- Where can those help?

A lawyer contributes differently than a graphic designer. Someone in a swing state contributes differently than someone in a safe state.

2. Existing capacity

   Ask:

- Who is already doing effective work on the issues I care about?
- How can I add to their capacity rather than duplicating their efforts?

Starting something new is hard. Joining existing efforts multiplies the impact of what is already happening.

3. Sustainability

   Ask:

- What is local and concrete enough for me to affect?
- What level of engagement can I maintain for years, not weeks?

National issues often feel most urgent, but local work may be where your efforts create visible change.

Better to commit to two hours a week consistently than to twenty hours a week until you collapse.

What feeds you? Some actions energize you; others drain you. Advocacy that requires confrontation might exhaust an introvert while energizing an extrovert. Work that involves helping individuals might sustain you better than abstract policy work, or vice versa. Choose forms of engagement you can do without hating every minute.

The Permission to Choose

Here is something hard to accept.

You are allowed not to work on everything.

You are allowed to focus. You are allowed to say, "Someone else will have to handle that," about issues that matter but are not your focus. This is not selfishness. This is effectiveness.

If everyone worked on everything superficially, nothing would receive the sustained attention it requires.

If people choose their focus and go deep, the collective effort covers more ground more efficiently.

You are one person. You get to choose where to give your one person's time.

Choose strategically.

Before You Move On

If you can identify one honest lever and one sustainable lane, this chapter has done its first job. You do not have to resolve the whole struggle before you can act with integrity.

The next chapter extends strategy into the longer work: culture, pacing, recovery, leverage, roles, and the choice to step back when doing so preserves future usefulness.

Chapter Fourteen: Acting With Strategy Over Time

Choosing a lane is the beginning of strategy, not the whole of it. The longer work raises another set of questions: what culture are we trying to keep alive, how do we pace ourselves, what action has leverage, what role fits, and when is stepping back the wiser move?

This chapter keeps action aligned with coherence. It helps you act without scattering, rest without shame, and remain useful without giving every outrage equal claim on your life.

How To Use This Chapter

Use this chapter when you have enough steadiness to think beyond the next reaction. It is especially useful if you are already active but feel burned out, unsure of where your effort matters, or caught in spaces that drain more than they build. Choose one section that fits your current decision. Strategy is meant to focus your care, not to make you colder. If a section clarifies one choice you need to make, that is enough for now.

When Culture Stops Giving Reliable Answers

Strategy is not only about choosing an issue or an organization. It is also about recognizing what kind of world you are trying to act within.

Antonovsky treated culture as one of the resources that help people maintain coherence.

A healthy culture gives people shared answers. It tells us what is normal, honorable, and shameful; what people owe one another; what is worth protecting; and how a decent person behaves when things get hard.

Those shared answers reduce the burden on each person. You do not have to invent everything from scratch. You can draw on the culture around you.

But in the current political process, culture itself is under attack.

That means some of the answers people used to rely on may no longer hold.

Old assumptions may fail:

- Institutions will protect the vulnerable.
- Cruelty disqualifies a leader.
- Facts will settle the argument.
- Most people will reject open harm after they see it.
- Decency will reassert itself.

When those answers stop working, the loss is not only political but also deeply disorienting. The reader is not only asking, "What should I do?"

The reader is also asking:

- What is still true?
- What kind of person am I trying to be?
- Who can I trust to think with me?
- Which answers are worth carrying forward?
- Which answers do we need to build now?

This is why isolated action is not enough. We need to develop and hold better answers alongside others who share our core values. That does not mean building a closed circle where everyone agrees on everything. It means refusing to let cruelty, confusion, and exhaustion define reality for us.

It means finding people committed to dignity, truth, protection, fairness, and care, then practicing those values together until they become more than private opinions. They form a small culture. This may be one of the long tasks ahead:

- Preserve the humane answers that remain true.
- Release the answers that no longer fit the moment.
- Build new answers with people who share similar values.

Practice those answers in families, friendships, neighborhoods, organizations, and local communities. Then pass them on.

Rebuilding culture sounds too large for one person. It is too large for one person. But culture is not rebuilt only by institutions. It is rebuilt when people repeatedly choose what to honor, protect, teach, refuse, and normalize. That makes culture work part of strategic engagement. Not every action has to be dramatic.

Sometimes the strategic act is to help a small group of people remember the kind of world they are trying to keep alive.

Pacing for the Long Haul

Once you have chosen where to focus, you need to pace yourself for sustained engagement. This means building practices that can endure for years, not just for one urgent season.

Use this section when your care is real but your rhythm is not yet sustainable. Pacing is not a lack of seriousness. It is how serious work survives. The goal is to keep showing up without treating your own collapse as proof of commitment.

Define Your Sustainable Commitment

Be specific.

Not "I'll do what I can."

Try:

- "I commit to four hours per week."
- "I'll attend the monthly meeting and take on one task between meetings."

The commitment should be something you can maintain even during difficult personal periods.

If your commitment assumes that everything in your life is going well, it will fail the first time you get sick, face a family crisis, or go through a difficult stretch at work.

You can always do more when you have more capacity. The baseline commitment is what you can sustain even during hard times.

Protect Your Recovery

Recovery is not a reward for after the work is finished. In the long run, recovery is part of the work. Use this practice when guilt tells you to keep going even though your body, judgment, or relationships are strained.

Build recovery into the plan before the next commitment.

Ask:

- What will this action cost me? What will help me come down afterward?
- Who can I be with, or what quiet do I need?
- What joy, sleep, food, movement, prayer, music, or ordinary life will restore me?

Then schedule one recovery step as seriously as you schedule the action. People who learn last to treat recovery as a requirement for continued usefulness, not as a treat.

Notice Your Warning Signs

Learn to recognize when you are heading toward burnout before you crash.

Common warning signs include:

- Physical signs: exhaustion that does not resolve with rest, increased susceptibility to illness, trouble sleeping, or changes in appetite. Emotional signs: persistent cynicism or hopelessness, irritability with allies, numbness, or dread when thinking about engagement.
- Behavioral signs: difficulty focusing, withdrawing from relationships, increased substance use, or going through the motions without being present.

When you notice these signs, take them seriously. Reduce your commitment, get support, and rest. It is better to pull back temporarily than to crash completely and be unable to continue.

Thinking Strategically

Strategy means thinking about how a step might help, not only whether it expresses your feelings. Use this when deciding where to spend time, money, attention, courage, or public voice.

The goal is not to become cold or calculating. The goal is to let your values find a path that can matter. If an action has no clear path to help, you may still choose it for witness, grief, solidarity, or conscience, but you should know which reason is guiding you.

Theory of Change

Before taking any action, ask two questions:

- What is my theory of change?
- How does this action lead to the outcome I want?

Sometimes the theory is plain.

For example:

I call my representative. My call is counted among thousands of others. The representative's staff reports constituent concerns, which may influence the representative's vote.

The connections are traceable.

Sometimes the theory is unclear: I post on social media and want to know whether it helps. I attend a march, and... something changes? These actions might still be valuable, but be honest with yourself about whether you understand how they create change or whether you are doing them just because they feel right. Feeling good is not wrong. But if you want to be effective, you need logical theories of change.

Leverage

Where can your effort have the greatest impact?

Some actions have high leverage. They generate more change per unit of effort.

Examples:

- Training others expands your impact.

- Building organizations creates capacity that endures beyond your individual input.
- Working on strategic bottlenecks moves things that otherwise would not move.

Some actions are lower-leverage. They may give you the feeling of doing something without creating much change.

Examples:

- Arguing with strangers online.
- Attending events that go nowhere. Consuming content about problems instead of working on solutions.

High leverage is not always possible.

Sometimes you can only do low-leverage work.

But when you can choose, choose leverage.

Playing Your Position

Ask:

What can I do that others cannot or are unlikely to do?

Your specific position in life may give you access, trust, or influence that others do not have.

For example:

You may work in an industry where your voice carries weight.

You may have relationships with people who need to hear certain messages. You may belong to a community where you can organize.

You may have financial resources you can use strategically.

The best action is not always the most visible action.

Sometimes the most useful action is the one your life makes possible.

When to Step Back

Strategic engagement includes knowing when not to engage. Use this section when action has started to cost more than it yields, when a space is harming you, or when your effort no longer has a credible path to usefulness.

Stepping back can mean several things. Name which one is true. You may be conserving energy for a better fight, recovering from depletion, or leaving a space that has become harmful. Those are different choices, and naming the difference helps you step back with less shame.

Disengaging from Futility

Some battles cannot be won right now. Some situations will not change no matter how much effort you put in. Some people will not be convinced no matter what you say. Recognizing futility is not giving up. It is conserving resources for fights that can be won. Pouring energy into genuinely hopeless situations is not heroic. It wastes strength needed elsewhere. This does not mean abandoning principles or accepting defeat. It means choosing where to fight based on where fighting can achieve something.

Disengaging for Recovery

Sometimes you need to step back, not because the fight is futile, but because you are drained.

Taking a break to recover is not abandoning the cause. It is ensuring you can return to it. If you are in burnout or heading there, allow yourself to step back temporarily. Others will hold the line while you recover. You'll be more useful when you come back than if you kept pushing through and collapsed.

Disengaging from Toxicity

Not all activist spaces are healthy. Some communities are rife with infighting, purity tests, callout culture, and other toxic dynamics that harm members while accomplishing little. If the space you are in is doing more harm than creating change, you are allowed to leave. Find healthier spaces. Create better alternatives. Or work independently for a while. You can be committed to the cause without being committed to a particular dysfunctional manifestation of it.

Finding Your Role

Movements, families, communities, and long struggles need many kinds of contributions. Use this section when you feel guilty because you are not doing the most visible thing, or when you are unsure where you fit.

Ask which role your life, skills, temperament, risk tolerance, and resources make possible right now. The right role is not always dramatic. It is the role you can carry with integrity and a chance of lasting.

The Visible Roles

Some people are suited to public-facing work: speaking, organizing, leading actions, and serving as the face of movements. This work is valuable, but it is not the only valuable work.

Choose this role only if it fits your gifts, risk tolerance, and season of life. Visibility can help the work, but it can also carry a cost. The right question is not who gets seen. The right question is what the work needs and what you can carry well.

The Supporting Roles

Behind every visible action lies invisible infrastructure. Someone makes the signs, books the venues, coordinates logistics, manages databases, writes grants, handles finances, provides childcare during meetings, and prepares food for volunteers.

This support work often matters more than the visible work. A movement with strong logistics can outlast one with charismatic leaders but no organization. If this is your role, do not call it minor.

The Care Roles

Some people serve movements by caring for those within them. They check on burned-out activists, provide emotional support, model sustainable engagement, and serve as a steady presence that helps others keep going.

This care work is often invisible and undervalued, but movements without it burn people out and collapse. If care is your role, protect it with boundaries so it endures. Caring for the people doing the work is one way to care for the work itself.

The Bridge Roles

Some people are positioned to bridge different worlds. They can speak to people on both sides of a divide. They have credibility in communities hostile to activists. They can translate messages for diverse audiences.

Bridge builders often face criticism from multiple sides. Still, they may be able to do work no one else can. If this is your role, stay clear about your values and do not confuse bridge-building with appeasement.

The Witness Roles

Some people contribute by documenting, remembering, and telling stories. Historians, journalists, and artists capture what is happening so it is not forgotten. This work often feels less urgent than direct action, but it matters in the long term. Movements need their stories told. What role fits you? It does not have to be the most visible or dramatic. It has to be something you can do well and sustainably.

Finding Sustainable Fire

After her burnout, Keisha took three months off from engagement. She felt guilty the entire time, but she was too exhausted to do anything else. When she returned, she was different. She chose one issue: voter access in her state. She joined an organization already doing good work. She committed to five hours a week, no more, with one weekend off each month. She noticed the old patterns creeping back: the urge to do more, attend more, and respond to every outrage.

She used her tools. She checked in with her community. She kept her commitment sustainable. A year later, she was still engaged. Her contributions had grown as she learned and built relationships, all within sustainable bounds. She'd helped register hundreds of voters.

She'd trained new volunteers who were now training others. Her work was creating ripples she'd never fully see. "I used to think engagement meant burning myself out," she said. "Now I know it means keeping my flame lit long enough to make a difference." James, who'd never burned out, had evolved as well. His consistent presence over the years had made him a leader in his organization, not because he sought leadership, but because people trusted him.

He'd been there through the ups and downs. He knew how things worked. New people looked to him for guidance. His five hours a week had grown into thousands over the years. His individual contribution had multiplied through everyone he'd helped develop. The organization was stronger because of his sustained presence. Neither Keisha nor James had changed the world. But both had changed their corner of it. And they were still changing it, week after week, year after year, because they'd learned to engage in ways they could sustain.

What Comes Next

You now have the tools to manage yourself, build community, and engage strategically with the problems you care about.

The next chapter turns this into a repeatable practice. It offers you a simple way to return to coherence when the next wave arrives.

After that, we will widen the frame again and consider the long game.

You may have come a long way since the overwhelm you started with. Now we make sure the work can be practiced, not just understood.

Before You Move On

Strategic engagement requires three things you can start building this week.

1. Name your lane.

Ask:

- Where do my specific skills fit?
- What time and energy do I truly have? Where am I genuinely useful?

Do not choose only by guilt.

Do not choose only by what is most visible.

Write one sentence:

"I am most useful when I..."

A clear lane prevents the exhausting, ineffective feeling of fighting on all fronts at once.

2. Set one specific goal for the next month.

Not an intention. A concrete action with a date.

Write:

"I will [specific thing] by [specific date]."

The specificity matters.

Vague intentions dissolve under pressure, while concrete commitments endure.

3. Schedule your recovery before your next commitment.

Not afterward. Before.

Before you agree to attend a meeting, make calls, or show up for an action, decide what you will do afterward to recharge.

Even ten minutes matters.

People who remain engaged over the years learn to view recovery as a requirement for continued usefulness, not as a reward.

You are not trying to do everything.

You are trying to do your part, well, for as long as it takes.

Chapter Fifteen: The Daily Practice

This chapter is where the book becomes repeatable. A good idea may help once. A practice helps you return when the next wave hits and your mind cannot recall everything you once understood.

The daily practice is deliberately small. It is not a test of discipline. It is a way to return to coherence in plain language: what is happening, what matters, and what I can do?

How To Use This Chapter

Use this chapter when you want a simple, repeatable way back to coherence. The daily practice is not a test of discipline. It is a way to ask, in plain language: what is happening, what matters, and what can I do? If the risk is concrete, begin with safety before reflection. If you are flooded, use the shorter version. The practice should fit your state today.

The Daily Practice

The daily practice is simple.

Three questions:

- What is happening?
- What matters?
- What can I do?

Those questions are the plain form of coherence. They help you understand enough, remember what the moment should serve, and find one possible action. But the practice should not feel the same every day. A person who is flooded does not need the same practice as a person who is worn down. A person facing concrete risk does not need a gentle reflection before safety. Use the version that fits your state today.

Why Practice At All

You have learned many tools in this book. You have learned to name feelings, steady your body, sort through pressure, check the information flood, map support, choose a sustainable lane, and return to what matters. That is a lot to remember. Under stress, people do not usually rise to the most elegant idea they once read. They reach for what is familiar. Daily practice makes the three questions familiar. Not perfect. Familiar.

The goal is not to become endlessly calm. The goal is to have a small doorway back when stress narrows the room.

The practice also helps you integrate what you are learning:

1. Identify: What is happening?
1. Analyze: What is this asking of me?
1. Generalize: What can I carry forward from this moment?

You do not need to use those words every day. The point is to turn experience into practical learning.

The Three Questions

Ask them plainly.

What Is Happening?

This question helps you make enough sense of the moment. It does not require a full explanation.

It may be as simple as:

- My body is flooded.
- I am grieving.
- I am tired.
- The news hit something tender.
- This is a real risk, not just a feeling. I do not know yet.

Even "I do not know yet" can be honest information.

What Matters?

This question helps you remember why the effort is worth making. The answer does not need to be grand.

It may be:

- My family.
- My health.
- My neighbor.
- My work.
- Democracy.
- The living world.
- My promise not to become cruel.

The person I am trying to protect. The future I still wish to serve.

Meaning often returns through contact. Touch one thing that matters. That is enough for today.

What Can I Do?

This question helps you identify one available action.

It may be small:

- Exhale.
- Put the phone down.
- Drink water.
- Write down what happened.
- Call someone.
- Check a reliable current resource.
- Rest for ten minutes.
- Take one step I can take.

The point is not control. The point is contact with agency.

If no action is obvious, ask:

Where is the nearest honest lever located?

Then choose one type of step:

- Act.
- Prepare.
- Connect.
- Recover.

Sometimes the honest answer is not a public action. Sometimes it is calling one person, saving one fact, resting before you break, or joining work already underway.

That still counts.

If You Are Overwhelmed Right Now

Keep the practice very short.

Ask:

- What is happening? My body or mind is flooded with it.
- What can I do? Exhale, find the room, name the feeling, and choose a next step.
- What matters? I only need enough stability for the next few minutes.

That is the whole practice. Do not make it bigger.

If you want a sentence, use this:

I do not have to solve my life right now. I need one steadier step.

If You Are Worn Down and Trying To Keep Going

The worn-down version is not about intensity. It is about recovery and return.

Ask:

- What is going on? I am carrying a long load.
- What matters? I want to keep my humanity intact as I keep going.
- What can I do? Restore one support and take one small life-support action.

Then choose one act in service of returning.

- Rest in service of strength.
- Eat in service of steadiness.
- Call a friend in service of connection.
- Do five minutes of work in service of not giving up.
- Step back from outrage in service of clearer action.
- Touch something ordinary in service of staying human.

You are not trying to earn rest. You are trying to stay available to life.

If You Are Directly At Risk

Start with safety. Do not turn this into a reflection exercise if the situation needs action.

Ask:

- What is happening? There may be concrete risk.
- What can I do?
- Check safety,
- Contact someone trusted,
- Document what matters, or
- Find current, reliable resources.

What matters? Protection, dignity, and clear action.

The question "What matters?" should not minimize the risk. It should clarify what you are protecting. If the risk is immediate, this book is not the next step. Safety comes first.

If You Are Supporting Someone Else

Use the questions without taking over.

Ask:

- What is happening? Someone else may be carrying more risk, grief, or pressure than I am.
- What matters? Their safety, dignity, privacy, and agency.
- What can I do? Offer concrete help and listen before acting.

Then make the offer specific:

- I can drive you.
- I can sit with you.
- I can help look up current information.
- I can check in at a specific time.
- I can help document what happened.
- I can make a call while you sit next to me.

Useful help is often smaller and more concrete than anxious help wants to be. Ask what would help today. Ask what not to say, share, or do.

If You Have Enough Steadiness to Reflect

Some days you will have more room. Use the same three questions with a little more depth.

Ask:

- What pattern am I noticing?
- What did I do that protected life, dignity, truth, or connection?
- What resource did I use this week?
- What resource do I need next?
- What needs to be released, parked, prepared, or shared?

This is where the daily practice connects with the Four-Box Reset. Some things need action. Some need preparation. Some need another person. Some need to be set aside for now.

The Weekly Version

Once a week, give the questions more room. You do not need a perfect ritual. Ten minutes is enough.

What Is Happening?

Ask:

What kind of week was this?

Which words fit? Flooded, worn down, steady, supported, isolated, angry, numb, hopeful, or some mix of these? What pattern do I see?

What Matters?

Ask:

What did I touch this week that still matters?

It might be:

- A person.
- A value.
- A place.
- A promise.
- A piece of work.
- A small act of care.

You are looking for contact, not a grand answer.

Keep touching what matters.

What Can I Do?

What is one small action that would help next week?

It may be:

- Rest.
- Preparation.
- A conversation.
- A boundary.
- Joining with others.
- Asking for help.
- Doing less of something that keeps hurting you.

Choose one.

When The Practice Feels Pointless

Some days the practice will feel thin.

You may ask, what is happening, and answer:

Everything feels terrible.

You may ask, what matters, and answer:

I do not know.

You may ask, what can I do, and answer:

Almost nothing.

That still counts.

You told the truth about where you are.

On those days, make the practice smaller:

> What is happening? This is a hard day.
>
> What matters? I am still here.

What can I do? One ordinary thing.

Sometimes that is the whole practice.

A Small Example

Sarah's phone buzzed with a news alert. Six months earlier, that sound would have taken the next hour. She would have opened the story, followed links, sent anxious messages, and ended up more frightened than informed. This time, she paused.

She asked:

- What is happening? This alert triggered my alarm system.

- What matters? I want to stay useful today, not just be activated.
- What can I do? I can read it later, or I can check one reliable source now and then stop.

She put the phone down for ten minutes. Nothing was resolved. But something had shifted. She had not handed the next hour over to the loudest signal. That is what practice can do. Not every time. Not perfectly. Often enough to matter.

The Point

The daily practice is not homework. It is a way to return when stress narrows the room and you cannot remember the whole book.

Again and again, ask:

- What is happening?
- What matters?
- What can I do?

That is coherence in plain clothes. You are not trying to hold every idea at once. You are keeping three questions close enough to spot when the next wave comes, and that is enough practice for one day.

Before You Move On

Try the practice once, on paper, before you need it.

1. What is happening?

Write one honest sentence about today.

2. What matters?

Name one thing the day should serve.

3. What can I do?

Choose one small action, or one person to contact.

Then put it where you will find it tomorrow. A practice you have already done once is easier to return to than one you have only read about.

Chapter Sixteen: The Long Game

The long game is not a demand to endure forever without rest. It is a broader frame for staying faithful when the work extends beyond one crisis, one election, one policy fight, or one season of your own life.

This chapter exists so the reader does not mistake discouragement for the end of the story. The work may be long, but it is not carried by one person. It is passed on, shared, renewed, and rebuilt.

How To Use This Chapter

Use this chapter when the work feels bigger than a single day, election, crisis, or season of your life. The purpose is not to demand endless endurance. It is to widen the frame so discouragement is not mistaken for the end of the story. Rest, handoff, joy, and community are part of the long game, not breaks from it. If this chapter feels too large today, read only one section and let the wider view return slowly.

The Long Game

Rosa had been an activist for fifty years. She had marched for civil rights in the sixties, organized against the Vietnam War, fought for women's equality in the seventies, resisted Reagan in the eighties, and pushed for LGBTQ+ rights through the nineties and beyond.

She had witnessed victories and defeats, progress and backlash, hope and despair. A young organizer, exhausted and demoralized after only two years, asked her how she had kept going for so long.

Rosa thought for a moment.

"I stopped expecting to win in my lifetime," she said.

The young woman looked confused. "Why keep fighting?" she asked.

"Because I'm not fighting for my lifetime," Rosa said. "I'm fighting for my grandchildren's lifetime and their grandchildren's. I'm part of a relay race, not a sprint. My job is to carry the baton as far as I can and hand it off stronger than I received it."

She smiled at the younger woman.

"The people who fought slavery did not live to see the Civil Rights Movement. The suffragists who fought for voting rights did not live to see women run for president. But without them, none of that would have happened." "How do you avoid getting discouraged?"

"Who says I do not? I get discouraged all the time, but discouragement is just a feeling. It comes and goes. The work continues regardless."

Rosa's story is common. Variations of it recur during difficult times in history.

Ordinary people realize that the world they thought they knew has changed, sometimes gradually, sometimes suddenly.

In these moments, the question is rarely whether life will return to perfect stability. The more immediate concern is how people stay grounded amid uncertainty.

This chapter is about that perspective: the long view that enables sustained engagement when the crisis is not ending anytime soon.

Expanding Your Time Horizon

Most of us operate on short time horizons.

What is happening today? What is coming this week? Maybe, if we are thinking strategically, what might happen this year?

Short time horizons make sense for daily life, but they are terrible for sustaining engagement with large, slow-moving problems.

If you measure your efforts against what changes today or this month, you'll always feel like you're failing.

Long-term thinking broadens the horizon.

Instead of asking "Will this action change things today?" you ask, "Will this action contribute to change over years or decades?" Instead of measuring success by what happens in your lifetime, you measure it by what you contribute to the longer arc. This is not giving up on near-term change. It is putting near-term setbacks in perspective. When you are playing a fifty-year game, a bad year does not mean the game is lost.

History Moves Slowly, Then Fast

If you look only at the surface of history, change can seem sudden. One day, slavery was legal in the United States. After generations of struggle and a civil war, it was not. One day, women were denied the vote by law. Then the Nineteenth

The Amendment was ratified in 1920, though many women still faced racist and discriminatory barriers to voting. One day, marriage equality seemed politically impossible. Then it became law.

Beneath each sudden change lay decades of slow work. People organized, educated, lost battles, shifted culture inch by inch, and built power that was not visible until it was. Abolitionists worked for generations before emancipation. Suffragists worked for decades before the Nineteenth Amendment. LGBTQ+ people and allies worked for decades before marriage equality seemed possible. In each case, many of those who started the work did not live to see it through. This pattern holds in both directions.

Progress can be reversed just as slowly. Rights won can be eroded, and gains can be lost. Democratic backsliding happens gradually, then suddenly. Those who resist backsliding, like those who built progress, often work on timescales longer than their own lives.

You Are Part of Something Larger

One of the deepest sources of sustainable meaning is recognizing you are part of a lineage.

People before you fought for the freedoms you inherited. People after you will inherit whatever you protect and build.

You are not starting from scratch, nor are you the end of the story.

This perspective is both humbling and empowering.

Humbling because you cannot do it all yourself. Empowering because you do not need to.

Your job is not to solve everything.

Your job is to contribute what you can during your time and to hand off something worth continuing to those who come after you. Think about the people who came before you in whatever struggle matters to you. They faced their own moments of despair and periods when progress seemed impossible. Many of them did not live to see the changes they worked for. Yet their efforts mattered. They moved things forward and kept possibilities alive. You are doing the same thing now.

Even when you cannot see the results, you are part of something that extends beyond your lifetime.

What You are Building for Tomorrow

When you adopt long-game thinking, your actions take on new meaning. You are not only responding to today's crisis but also building for the future.

Use this section to ask what your effort may leave behind: people, culture, infrastructure, resilience, stories, habits, and ways of living for someone else to inherit. This can make small, faithful acts feel less isolated from the larger story.

Building People

Perhaps the most valuable long-term contribution is developing others.

That may mean:

- Training new activists.
- Mentoring the next generation.

- Raising children with strong values. Helping others build their resilience and capacity.

Every person you help develop becomes someone who can carry on the work when you cannot.

Your influence multiplies through the people you have shaped.

This is how movements sustain themselves across generations, not through institutions alone but through people who pass on knowledge, skills, and commitment to others.

Rebuilding Culture

Antonovsky described culture as our source of "magic answers." When culture is healthy, it can be easier to function, maintain coherence, and move toward health.

In the U.S., several pressures have eroded our culture:

- Too much power given to wealth. Corporate profits treated as the government's main goal.
- Media-driven division.
- The erosion of shared responsibility.

When culture is damaged, answers become much more of an individual responsibility. That becomes another stressor.

Rebuilding culture will be critical if we are to reverse current trends.

Culture is the water we swim in. It comprises the shared assumptions, values, and beliefs that shape how people view the world.

Cultural change is slow, yet it is what makes other changes possible.

Every conversation you have, every example you set, and every story you tell contributes to the culture.

You are not just influencing the person in front of you. You are contributing to a broader shift in what people consider normal, acceptable, and possible.

Cultural work often feels intangible compared with policy fights or electoral campaigns.

But it is the foundation on which everything else rests.

Building Infrastructure

Infrastructure is what endures when individuals come and go.

It includes organizations, institutions, networks, systems, and practices that can be passed down to those who come next. When you build an organization, create a mutual aid network, establish a practice, document what you have learned, or create resources others can use, you are building infrastructure.

Your contribution outlasts your personal involvement. That matters because long-term work cannot depend solely on whoever has energy this month.

Building Resilience

Your resilience is itself a contribution.

By staying strong during difficult times, you become a role model and a resource for others.

By not burning out, you remain available to help when help is needed.

Everything you have learned in this book, including the tools, practices, and perspectives, better equips you to play the long game.

Your resilience is the foundation for whatever else you contribute.

Maintaining Hope Without Expectations

Long-term thinking requires a particular relationship to hope and expectation.

If hope means expecting things to improve soon, you'll be disappointed. The timeline for change rarely aligns with our expectations.

Things often worsen before they improve, and "better" may never arrive in your lifetime.

But there is another kind of hope: hope as commitment rather than as expectation.

This hope says:

I will act as if positive change is possible, not because I am certain it will happen, but because acting that way is the only way to bring it about.

This kind of hope does not depend on evidence that things are improving. It persists even when conditions are worsening.

It is not optimism about outcomes. It is a commitment to a direction.

Vaclav Havel, who spent years as a dissident before becoming president of Czechoslovakia, wrote about this distinction.

Hope, he said, "is not the same as joy that things are going well, or willingness to invest in enterprises that are obviously headed for early success, but rather an ability to work for something because it is good, not just because it stands a chance to succeed." This kind of hope can coexist with a realistic assessment of how bad things are. You do not have to pretend that things are better than they are.

You must keep acting in line with what you believe is right.

The Practices That Sustain the Long Game

The long game requires practice, not just perspective. Use these when discouragement has narrowed your time horizon or when you need help staying connected to why the work is still worth doing.

Choose one practice at a time. The goal is not to become endlessly inspired. It is to keep returning to sources of strength that endure beyond a single burst of urgency.

Celebrate Small Victories

When you are playing a long game, you cannot wait for final victory to feel good about your efforts. You need to notice and celebrate the small wins along the way.

- A successful meeting.
- A person whose mind you shifted.
- A skill you developed.
- A relationship you deepened.
- A local battle you won.

These matter not because they are the end goal but because they are evidence that your efforts have an impact. Celebrating small victories is not naive optimism. It is a strategic way to replenish the motivation you need to keep going.

Remember the Wins

History is not only a story of oppression and defeat. It is also a story of victories once thought impossible. Women gained the right to vote. Slavery was abolished.

Child labor was outlawed. Workers won the eight-hour day. LGBTQ+ people won marriage equality. None of these changes seemed possible before they happened. When despair tells you change is impossible, remember what has already changed. The people who achieved those changes were no more capable than you. They just kept working longer than seemed reasonable.

Stay Connected to Joy

You cannot sustain engagement for decades on anger and fear alone.

You need sources of joy that remind you of what you are fighting for and replenish your capacity to keep going.

Joy is not a betrayal of the struggle. It is what sustains the struggle.

The people who burned brightest with righteous anger often burned out the fastest. The people who stayed the course were often those who knew how to laugh, love, and experience beauty even in dark times.

Make joy a practice, not an afterthought. Integrate it deliberately into your life.

Find Your Elders

Seek out people who have been doing this longer than you have.

Their perspective can be invaluable. They've seen cycles you haven't.

They know what it is like to work for years without visible progress, only to see things shift suddenly.

They understand despair as a phase, not a conclusion.

If you do not know long-term activists personally, read their memoirs, listen to their interviews, and study their lives.

Let their experience inform your understanding of what is possible.

Be an Elder for Others

Whatever experience you have is valuable to those with less. Even if you have been engaged for only a year or two, you know things that someone just starting out does not. Share what you have learned. Mentor those who come after you.

Be the steady presence that helps newcomers avoid burnout. Movements sustain themselves not just through institutions but through the personal transmission of knowledge, wisdom, and endurance.

When It Feels Like Too Much

Even with a long-term perspective, there will be times when it all feels like too much. When you want to give up. When despair is more than a passing feeling. When that happens, remember:

You do not have to do everything. You are one person contributing to a collective effort that spans generations.

Your job is to do your part, not to carry the entire load.

The rest is part of the work. Taking time to recover is not abandoning the struggle. It is ensuring you can return to it.

Movements need people who endure, not people who burn out heroically.

Despair is information, not a conclusion. When you feel hopeless, it means you are depleted or overwhelmed. It does not mean that hope is unreasonable.

Use your tools, seek support, and wait for the feeling to pass.

The work continues without you. If you need to step back for a time, others will hold the line. You can rejoin when you are able.

The movement is bigger than any individual.

Your very survival is a victory.

When powerful forces seek to demoralize and disengage you, simply continuing to care is resistance. Keeping your spirit intact is an achievement.

The Choice to Continue

Playing the long game is a choice you make again and again, not once but every day.

Not from certainty of success, but from a commitment to values that matter, regardless of the outcome.

You choose to continue even when progress is not visible. You choose to contribute even when your contribution seems invisible. You choose to stay engaged even when engagement is costly.

This choice is meaningful in itself.

It is a statement about the kind of person you want to be, the kind of world you want to help create, and what you believe is worth your limited time on Earth.

You may not live to see the change you are working for.

But the people who eventually see it will stand on the foundation you helped build.

They will inherit the culture you helped shape, the people you helped develop, and the infrastructure you helped build.

Your contribution matters, even if you never see its full effects. That is the nature of the long game, and of any effort that spans more than a single lifetime.

Looking Back, Looking Forward

You may have started this book feeling overwhelmed and anxious, struggling to cope with circumstances that felt impossible to bear.

You have learned why you feel the way you do: that your distress is an appropriate response to genuine threats, not a personal failing.

You have built tools to manage your internal state, process information, and remain grounded amid chaos.

You have developed strategies to build community and engage effectively with the issues you care about.

You have connected with sources of meaning that can sustain you through prolonged hardship.

Now you have the long view.

Your individual struggles are part of a larger story that extends backward and forward in time.

You are not alone. You are part of a lineage of people who have faced their own dark times and found ways to keep moving forward.

You are connected to a community of people who are facing similar challenges today.

You are contributing to a future that people not yet born will inherit.

Three Things to Carry

The long game is not only a perspective. It is a practice: something you must return to, deliberately, over time.

Once a month, look for one piece of evidence that the long game is being played.

It might be:

- A story about someone who kept going despite no visible results.
- A change that took a generation to achieve. A movement that seemed dead, then was not.

Let it remind you that you are part of something with a timeline longer than your own discouragement.

Write a letter to yourself to open in one year.

Keep it short. A paragraph or two is sufficient.

Ask yourself:

- What am I hoping for?
- What am I afraid of?
- What do I want to remember about this moment?
- Who am I trying to be in it?

Seal the letter.

Put it somewhere you will find it.

What you write may surprise you when you read it later.

If you want to make the commitment less private, tell one trusted person what you wrote.

Not to recruit them.

Not to convince them.

Just to let one other person know what you are trying to hold on to.

This act of witness, of being known for your effort, is not a small thing. It changes the texture of the work.

The crisis is not over. It may never end in your lifetime.

But you are not the same person who began reading this book.

You are stronger now. More grounded. Better equipped. Part of something bigger than yourself.

That is what staying strong means.

Not never feeling weak.

Not having all the answers.

Not being certain of victory.

Just showing up day after day, contributing what you can to the ongoing human project of building a world worth living in.

A Final Reflection

If you have read this far, you have likely recognized something many people are beginning to sense but cannot always articulate clearly. The strain many of us feel right now is not simply personal stress. It stems from living in a period when the systems that normally provide stability and predictability feel less reliable than they once did. When that happens, people naturally experience more confusion, more anger, and more fatigue.

Aaron Antonovsky spent much of his career trying to understand why some people remain relatively healthy under difficult conditions while others become overwhelmed. His conclusion was surprisingly simple. People do better when life feels understandable, when they believe they have at least some ability to influence their circumstances, and when their efforts still feel meaningful. When those elements weaken, the pressure on the body and mind increases quickly. One of this book's goals has been to help restore those elements where we can.

Sometimes it begins with very practical steps: settling the nervous system when it becomes overloaded, limiting the constant stream of alarming information, and rebuilding the kinds of relationships that help people regain their footing. None of these steps remove the larger problems we are living with. They simply make it easier to remain steady while those problems continue to unfold. Viktor Frankl observed something similar under much harsher conditions.

Even in the most extreme environments, he found that people were better able to endure when they could still find meaning in how they responded to their circumstances. Meaning did not remove suffering, but it often changed how people carried it.

Most of us will never face the conditions Frankl described, but the principle remains useful. When circumstances become uncertain, the question of how we live through them grows more pressing. For some, the answer will involve quiet acts of care within families and communities. For others, it may involve defending institutions, helping vulnerable groups, or participating in the slow work of repairing what has been damaged. There is no single right role.

What matters is that we do not allow confusion, anger, or fear to narrow our lives to the point that we lose the ability to think clearly or act with care toward others. The practices described in these pages are simply tools to help us return to that steadiness when it begins to slip.

Because it will slip.

Periods of social strain rarely move in straight lines. They surge and settle, improve and worsen, often over longer stretches than people expect.

Maintaining coherence under those conditions is not a one-time accomplishment. It is something people rebuild repeatedly, again and again, if necessary.

History suggests that the conditions we are living through will eventually change.

In the meantime, the task facing most of us is more immediate and more personal.

To keep our footing. To remain connected to one another. And, as best we can, to stay strong in unsteady times.

Current Resources

How To Use Current Resources

Some help ages well. Breathing, grounding, naming what you feel, asking for support, and choosing one next step will still matter years from now. Other help changes. Laws, policies, technology, and local resources change. What is safe in one place may not be safe in another. Use this page as a map. Do not use it as legal, medical, crisis, or security advice.

If There Is Immediate Danger

If someone is in immediate danger, use trusted people and appropriate local help. Do not try to resolve immediate danger on your own. If you may harm yourself or someone else, or if you cannot stay safe, reach out to a trusted person, local crisis support, emergency care, or a qualified professional. A book can help you slow down. A book should not be the only help you use when safety is at stake.

United States starting points checked during this revision:

- Immediate emergency: call 911.
- Suicide, crisis, or emotional distress in the United States: call or text 988. Chat: https://988lifeline.org/chat/. Website: https://988lifeline.org.
- Text-based crisis support: text HOME to 741741. Website: https://www.crisistextline.org/. Domestic violence, relationship abuse, or coercive control: National Domestic Violence Hotline, 800.799.SAFE. Text START to 88788. Website: https://www.thehotline.org/.

Resource check date: August 31, 2026.

If you are outside the United States, use current resources where you live.

If someone may be monitoring your internet use, be careful when visiting safety websites. The National Domestic Violence Hotline notes that internet use can be monitored and may not be completely erased. If that may apply to you, calling from a safer phone may be better than browsing.

Civil Rights, Protest, Immigration, And Public Systems

When rights, immigration, protest, school, workplace, medical access, or public-system issues arise, consult current sources. Start with trusted civil-liberties groups, official agencies, local advocates, or qualified professionals.

Before relying on a page, ask:

- When was it updated?
- Does it apply where I live?
- Is this general information or actual advice for my situation?

Do I need a local lawyer, advocate, provider, union, or organization? Could the safest next step depend on details this page does not know?

Useful places to check:

- ACLU Know Your Rights:
- https://www.aclu.org/know-your-rights ACLU Protesters' Rights: https://www.aclu.org/know-your-rights/protesters-rights ACLU LGBTQ rights tracker:
  https://www.aclu.org/legislative-attacks-on-lgbtq-rights-2026
- EEOC Filing A Charge of Discrimination: https://www.eeoc.gov/filing-charge-discrimination

These resources are starting points. They are not a substitute for local guidance when the risk is concrete.

Online Security And Privacy

Digital safety depends on your situation. The right step for one person may pose a risk for another. Before changing accounts, phones, passwords, apps, or devices, ask:

- What am I trying to protect?
- Who might try to access it?
- What would happen if they did?

What tools do I already use? What change would make me safer without making daily life unmanageable? Could a sudden change alert someone to an unsafe situation?

Useful places to check:

- EFF Surveillance Self-Defense:

https://ssd.eff.org/ NNEDV Safety Net Project: https://nnedv.org/content/technology-safety/

- Safety Net: https://www.techsafety.org/

The safest tool is not always the most complex. The safest step is often the one that matches the real threat and can be sustained.

Documentation

If something happened and it is safe to document, write down:

- Date
- Time
- Place
- What happened
- Who was involved
- Who saw it
- What records exist
- Where copies are stored

Keep it plain. Do not guess. Do not exaggerate. If documentation could increase your risk, pause and seek safer guidance.

A Simple Source Check

Before trusting a resource, ask:

- Who made this?
- What do they know?
- When was it updated?
- Does it apply to my place?

  Does it clearly state what it can and cannot do? Is someone trying to scare me, sell me something, or rush me?

Good help does not need to panic you. It makes the next step clearer.

What This Book Can and Can't Do

This book can help you slow down, make sense of the situation, name what matters, and choose the next step. It can help you remember that you do not have to carry everything alone. It can help you ask better questions. But when the risk is concrete, current help matters. Use the book to steady yourself. Use current resources to guide action.

Sources And Technique Notes

This book draws on several streams of work. Some are research frameworks. Some are clinical or public health practices translated into plain language. Some are my own synthesis of tools I have used, taught, revised, and tested over years of work with people under pressure. I have tried to be clear about the distinction.

Coherence And Salutogenesis

The central idea of coherence stems from Aaron Antonovsky's salutogenic model of health. Antonovsky asked why some people can move toward health even under serious stress. His answer centered on a sense of coherence: the felt experience that life is at least somewhat understandable, that resources are available, and that effort still has meaning. In this book, I translate that into three plain questions:

- Can I understand enough?
- Does this still matter?
- Can I do something?

The plain-language form is my adaptation, while the deeper frame belongs to Antonovsky's work.

The Generalized Resistance Resources language also derives from Antonovsky's salutogenic model. The list in Chapter One is a reader-facing translation, not a clinical measure.

Sources:

- Antonovsky, A. (1979). Health, Stress, and Coping. Jossey-Bass. Antonovsky, A. (1987). Unraveling the Mystery of Health. Jossey-Bass. Sense of Coherence, NCBI Bookshelf: https://www.ncbi.nlm.nih.gov/books/NBK585678/
- Generalized Resistance Resources in the Salutogenic Model of Health, NCBI Bookshelf: https://www.ncbi.nlm.nih.gov/books/NBK584114/
- Specific Resistance Resources in the Salutogenic Model of Health, NCBI Bookshelf: https://www.ncbi.nlm.nih.gov/books/NB K584066/

Culture And Shared Answers

The material on culture as a source of shared answers is also grounded in Antonovsky's salutogenic framework. In that framework, cultural stability, social belonging, institutional support, values, and shared meanings can serve as resources that help people maintain coherence under stress. The book's language about "built-in answers" and rebuilding humane answers with people of similar values is my adaptation.

The source frame is Antonovsky's work on generalized resistance resources and the sense of coherence.

Sources:

- Antonovsky, A. (1979). Health, Stress, and Coping. Jossey-Bass.

- Antonovsky, A. (1987). Unraveling the Mystery of Health. Jossey-Bass.

Meaning And The Long Game

The book's meaning material is deeply shaped by Viktor Frankl's work, especially Man's Search for Meaning and his later writings on tragic optimism. The book does not use meaning to excuse harm, explain who survives atrocity, or pressure people to find growth in suffering. It uses meaning as one source of fuel for staying human under strain.

Sources:

- Frankl, V. E. (2006). Man's Search for Meaning. Beacon Press.
- Frankl, V. E. The Case for a Tragic Optimism, published as a postscript in the 2006 Beacon Press edition of Man's Search for Meaning.
- Viktor Frankl Institute, Biography: https://www.viktorfrankl.org/biography.h tml
- Online Archive of California, Viktor Frankl Collection: https://oac.cdlib.org/findaid/ark:/13030/ tf7g5005bh

First Help Under Stress

The opening structure of this book draws on public health and disaster recovery approaches that emphasize humane, practical, low-pressure support. The goal is not to force insight. The goal is to help a person regain enough steadiness to take the next right step.

Sources:

- World Health Organization, War Trauma Foundation, and World Vision International. (2011). Psychological First Aid: Guide for Field Workers. https://www.who.int/publications/i/item /9789241548205
- Berkowitz, S., Bryant, R., Brymer, M., Hamblen, J., Jacobs, A., Layne, C., Macy, R., Osofsky, H., Pynoos, R., Ruzek, J.,

- Steinberg, A., Vernberg, E., and Watson, P. (2010). Skills for Psychological Recovery: Field Operations Guide. https://www.ptsd.va.gov/disaster_events/ for_providers/skills_psych_recovery.asp Hobfoll, S. E., et al. (2007). Five Essential
  Elements of Immediate and Mid-Term Mass Trauma Intervention: Empirical Evidence. Psychiatry, 70(4), 283-315. https://doi.org/10.1521/psyc.2007.70.4.2
  83

Breathing And Body Tools

The two-inhale breath used in this book is a plain-language version of a pattern often called the physiological sigh or cyclic sighing. Breathing tools can help reduce acute arousal for many people. They do not make danger disappear. They do not replace safety, medical care, crisis support, or another person when those are needed.

Sources:

- Balban, M. Y., et al. (2023). Brief structured respiration practices enhance mood and reduce physiological arousal.
  Cell Reports Medicine, 4(1), 100895.
  https://doi.org/10.1016/j.xcrm.2022.1008
  95
- Skills for Psychological Recovery, especially the managing reactions material.

Grounding And Orienting

The grounding tools in this book, including finding the room and using the senses, are adapted from practices for grounding and managing reactions used in trauma, anxiety, and disaster-recovery settings. The purpose is modest. Grounding helps many people return their attention to the present moment. It does not prove that someone is safe.

Sources:

- Skills for Psychological Recovery: https://www.ptsd.va.gov/disaster_events/for_providers/skills_psych_recovery.asp Skills for Psychological Recovery Field Operations Guide PDF: https://www.nctsn.org/sites/default/files/resources/specialresource/spr_complete_english.pdf

STOP And Pause Skills

The STOP tool is adapted from Dialectical Behavior Therapy skills. In this book, it is presented as a simple pause sequence, not as a full clinical intervention or a substitute for therapy, crisis help, medical care, or safety planning.

Sources:

- Linehan, M. M. (2015). DBT Skills Training Handouts and Worksheets (2nd ed.). Guilford Press. STOP Skill, DBT.tools: https://dbt.tools/emotional_regulation/st op.php

Butterfly Hug

The Butterfly Hug is associated with EMDR-related bilateral stimulation practices. In this book, it is offered modestly as a settling option that some people may find useful. It should be presented as optional, and readers should stop if it feels uncomfortable or irritating.

Sources:

- Francine Shapiro Library, The EMDR Therapy Butterfly Hug Method: https://francineshapirolibrary.omeka.net/items/show/27518
- Jarero, I., and Artigas, L. (2010). The EMDR Integrative Group Treatment Protocol: Application with child victims of a mass disaster. Journal of EMDR Practice and Research.

Naming Feelings

The "name the feeling" tool is a plain-language version of affect labeling. Putting a feeling into words can help reduce its grip and make the next step clearer. Naming a feeling does not make it disappear. It helps turn the feeling into information.

Sources:

- Lieberman, M. D., et al. (2007). Putting Feelings Into Words: Affect Labeling Disrupts Amygdala Activity in Response to Affective Stimuli. Psychological Science, 18(5), 421-428. https://doi.org/10.1111/j.1467-9280.2007.01916.x

Feelings As Signals

The feelings map in Chapter Two is not a diagnostic system. It is a plain-language guide to listening. The idea is simple: emotions can convey useful information about danger, loss, violated values, overload, shame, exhaustion, love, and the need for support. They still require discernment. A feeling may be honest without being the full assessment.

The material on grief covers ordinary grief and broader forms of grief, including grief over a country, a future, a community, a way of life, or harm to the natural world. The material on overwhelm treats overload as a capacity signal, not a character flaw.

Sources:

- Hwang, H., and Matsumoto, D. Functions of Emotions. Noba Project. https://nobaproject.com/modules/functions-of-emotions

- Schwarz, N. (2012). Feelings-asinformation theory. In Handbook of Theories of Social Psychology. Sage. Summary page: https://dornsife.usc.edu/norbert-schwarz/feeling-thinking/
- American Psychological Association. Grief. https://www.apa.org/topics/grief Cunsolo, A., and Ellis, N. R. (2018). Ecological grief as a mental health response to climate

change-related loss. Nature Climate Change, 8, 275-281. https://doi.org/10.1038/s41558-018-
0092-2

- Comtesse, H., Ertl, V., Hengst, S. M. C., Rosner, R., and Smid, G. E. (2021).
Ecological Grief as a Response to
Environmental Change: A Mental Health Risk or Functional Response? International Journal of Environmental Research and Public Health, 18(2), 734. https://doi.org/10.3390/ijerph18020734
- Arnold, M., Goldschmitt, M., and Rigotti, T. (2023). Dealing with information overload: a comprehensive review. Frontiers in Psychology, 14, 1122200.
https://doi.org/10.3389/fpsyg.2023.11222
00
- Lazarus, R. S., and Folkman, S. (1984).
Stress, Appraisal, and Coping. Springer.

Hate, Helplessness, And Reader Power

The hate chapter treats hate as distinct from anger. The body text uses plain language and does not ask readers to forgive, excuse harm, or compromise moral clarity. The point is to help readers translate hate into protection, accountability, lawful action, connection, and recovery.

The chapter also distinguishes between control and influence. This is Ray's reader-facing adaptation of research on collective action, agency, and shared efficacy. The plain-language tool is the "nearest honest lever." It is not a clinical protocol.

Sources:

- Fischer, A. H., Halperin, E., Canetti, D., and Jasini, A. (2018). Why We Hate.
Emotion Review. https://doi.org/10.1177/175407391775122
9

- Martinez, C. A., et al. (2022). Hate: Toward understanding its distinctive features across interpersonal and intergroup targets. Emotion. https://pubmed.ncbi.nlm.nih.gov/349681 44/
- Halperin, E., Russell, A. G., Dweck, C. S., and Gross, J. J. (2011). Anger, Hatred, and the Quest for Peace: Anger Can Be Constructive in the Absence of Hatred. Journal of Conflict Resolution. https://doi.org/10.1177/00220027103836 70
- Harel, T. O., Jameson, J. K., and Maoz, I. (2020). The Normalization of Hatred: Identity, Affective Polarization, and Dehumanization on Facebook in the Context of Intractable Political Conflict. Social Media + Society. https://doi.org/10.1177/20563051209139 83
- Dangerous Speech Project. Dangerous Speech: A Practical Guide. https://www.dangerousspeech.org/librari es/guide
- National Center for PTSD. Moral Injury. https://www.ptsd.va.gov/professional/tre at/cooccurring/moral_injury.asp van Zomeren, M., Postmes, T., and Spears, R. (2008). Toward an integrative social identity model of collective action: A quantitative research synthesis of three socio-psychological perspectives. Psychological Bulletin. https://doi.org/10.1037/0033-2909.134.4.504
- Yale School of Public Health. (2022). Collective action helps young adults deal with climate change anxiety. https://ysph.yale.edu/newsarticle/collective-action-helps-youngadults-deal-with-climate-change-anxiety/ AP-NORC Center for Public Affairs

Research. AP-NORC Public Opinion Trends. Checked August 25, 2026. https://apnorc.org/projects/ap-norc-polling-trends/

- AP-NORC Center for Public Affairs Research. Fewer approve of Trump's handling of the economy. April 2026. https://apnorc.org/projects/fewerapprove-of-trumps-handling-of-theeconomy/
- Associated Press. Why immigration remains strong for Trump among Republicans, according to a new APNORC poll. August 2026. https://apnews.com/article/trumpapproval-rating-immigration-economyiran-healthcare-
- f14da4276e2e0d5ec9b79f0d48e22788 Marist Poll. The Actions of ICE, February 2026.
- https://maristpoll.marist.edu/polls/the-actions-of-ice-february-2026/ Marist Poll. It is Trump's Economy and Americans Are Not Impressed, June 2026. https://maristpoll.marist.edu/polls/itstrumps-economy-and-americans-are-notimpressed-june-2026/
- Pew Research Center. Trump Gets Negative Reviews Internationally as Fewer Say U.S. Is a Reliable Partner. June 23, 2026. https://www.pewresearch.org/global/2026/06/23/trump-gets-negative-reviewsinternationally-as-fewer-say-u-s-is-areliable-partner/

Unhooking From Thoughts

The "unhook from the loudest thought" tool is a plain-language adaptation of cognitive defusion from Acceptance and Commitment Therapy. ACT does not ask people to erase difficult thoughts and feelings before acting. Instead, it helps people notice their inner experience and still move in the direction of their chosen values.

Sources:

- Association for Contextual Behavioral Science, The Six Core Processes of ACT: https://contextualscience.org/six_core_processes_act
- Hayes, S. C., Strosahl, K. D., and Wilson, K. G. (2011). Acceptance and Commitment Therapy: The Process and Practice of Mindful Change (2nd ed.). Guilford Press.

Life-Support Action

The "life-support action" tool is a plain-language adaptation of behavioral activation, positive activity scheduling, and committed action. The point is not forced positivity. Small, purposeful action can come before motivation fully returns.

Sources:

- Society of Clinical Psychology, Behavioral Activation for Depression: https://societyofclinicalpsychology.org/psychological-treatmentsarchive/behavioral-activation-fordepression/
- NICE guideline NG222, Depression in adults: treatment and management: https://www.nice.org.uk/guidance/ng222 /chapter/recommendations
- Skills for Psychological Recovery, promoting positive activities.

Self-Compassion And Self-Attack

The tool called "stop adding self-attack" is a practical expression of self-compassion. It is not sentimental. It is a way to stop adding shame to an already heavy load.

Sources:

- Han, A., and Kim, T. H. (2023). Effects of Self-Compassion Interventions on Reducing Depressive Symptoms, Anxiety, and Stress: A Meta-Analysis. Mindfulness, 14, 1553-1581. https://pubmed.ncbi.nlm.nih.gov/37362192/

- Neff, K. D. (2003). Self-Compassion: An Alternative Conceptualization of a Healthy Attitude Toward Oneself. Self and Identity, 2(2), 85-101. https://doi.org/10.1080/1529886030903 2

Sustainable Action And Burnout

The sustainable-lane tools are informed by burnout, pacing, limits, and committed action. The book should frame burnout as a warning of sustained load and depleted capacity, not as a personal failure or a fixed identity.

Sources:

- Maslach, C., and Leiter, M. P. (2016). Understanding the Burnout Experience: Recent Research and Its Implications for Psychiatry. World Psychiatry, 15(2), 103111. https://pubmed.ncbi.nlm.nih.gov/272656 91/
- World Health Organization. Burn-out an occupational phenomenon: International Classification of Diseases. https://www.who.int/standards/classifica tions/frequently-asked-questions/burnout-an-occupational-phenomenon

Sustained Load On The Body And Brain

The discussion of old tools losing power under sustained strain draws on allostatic load research. The body text uses plain language rather than that term. The point is simple: repeated or long-term stress can increase the cost borne by the body and brain. This does not mean the reader is broken. It means the load has changed.

Sources:

- McEwen, B. S., and Stellar, E. (1993). Stress and the Individual: Mechanisms Leading to Disease. Archives of Internal Medicine, 153(18), 2093-2101.

https://pubmed.ncbi.nlm.nih.gov/837980
0/

Worry, Rumination, And Uncertainty

The information-flood tools draw on research on worry, rumination, intolerance of uncertainty, doomscrolling, and attention loops. The book translates this into monitoring windows, worry limits, the question before opening the feed, the output rule, and returning to one useful action.

Sources:

- McCarrick, D., Prestwich, A., Prudenzi, A., and O'Connor, D. B. (2021). Health Effects of Psychological Interventions for Worry and Rumination: A Meta-Analysis.
  https://pubmed.ncbi.nlm.nih.gov/344107
  60/
- Miller, M. L., and McGuire, J. F. (2023). Targeting Intolerance of Uncertainty in Treatment: A Meta-Analysis.
  https://pubmed.ncbi.nlm.nih.gov/376576
  23/
  Gentes, E. L., and Ruscio, A. M. (2011). A Meta-Analysis of the Relation of Intolerance of Uncertainty to Symptoms of Generalized Anxiety Disorder, Major Depressive Disorder, and ObsessiveCompulsive Disorder.
  https://pubmed.ncbi.nlm.nih.gov/216643
  39/
- UC San Diego Today. (2025). Doomscrolling Again? Expert Explains Why We are Wired for Worry. https://today.ucsd.edu/story/doomscrolli ng-again-expert-explains-why-werewired-for-worry
- Mental Health Foundation. (2025). Doomscrolling: tips for healthier news consumption.

https://www.mentalhealth.org.uk/explore -mental-health/articles/doomscrollingtips-healthier-news-consumption

Information Manipulation And Firehosing

The information-flood and drift material draws on research in misinformation inoculation and prebunking. The body text uses plainer language to explain manipulation, pattern recognition, and information flooding. The goal is not cynicism. The goal is discernment, especially when fear, outrage, and exhaustion make manipulation easier.

The firehosing language is grounded in RAND's "firehose of falsehood" model. The book uses the term more generally to describe high-volume information flooding that exhausts attention and makes judgment harder.

The coherence-sabotage language is this book's synthesis. Antonovsky supplies the coherence frame. Information overload, misinformation, disinformation, propaganda, and firehosing research help explain how confusing, high-volume, emotionally loaded, or false information can make reality harder to sort out, trust harder to place, and action harder to choose.

Do not claim that every false statement is an act of intentional sabotage. Misinformation can spread when people are mistaken.

Disinformation and propaganda involve more deliberate influence. The reader-facing point is that all three can weaken coherence, especially when people are already afraid, angry, exhausted, or directly at risk.

Sources:

- Psychological Inoculation for Credibility

  Assessment, Sharing Intention, and Discernment of Misinformation: A MetaAnalysis. https://pmc.ncbi.nlm.nih.gov/articles/PMC10498317/

Paul, C., and Matthews, M. (2016). The Russian "Firehose of Falsehood" Propaganda Model. RAND Corporation. https://www.rand.org/pubs/perspectives/PE198.html

Community And Support

The Support Map is my synthesis, but it draws on well-established work on social support, social connection, and recovery after adversity. The role categories in this book are not copied from a single source. They are a practical map for asking: who helps me get steady, think, act, understand the stakes, stay connected to meaning, and avoid carrying risk alone?

Sources:

- Skills for Psychological Recovery, healthy social connections.
- Holt-Lunstad, J., Smith, T. B., and Layton, J. B. (2010). Social Relationships and Mortality Risk: A Meta-Analytic Review. https://pubmed.ncbi.nlm.nih.gov/206686
59/
- Coan, J. A., and Sbarra, D. A. (2015). Social Baseline Theory: The Social Regulation of Risk and Effort. https://pmc.ncbi.nlm.nih.gov/articles/PMC4375548/

Zagic, D., et al. (2022). Interventions to improve social connections: a systematic review and meta-analysis. https://pubmed.ncbi.nlm.nih.gov/347963
68/

Social Movements And Historical Examples

The social-movement examples are intended to help readers think about time, contribution, and collective action. They should avoid lone-hero simplification. Rosa Parks' refusal was historically consequential because it became part of a sustained boycott and built on years of organizing. The suffrage example should use "suffragists" in the U.S. context and note that the Nineteenth Amendment did not remove all barriers to voting.

Sources:

- King Institute, Montgomery Bus Boycott: https://kinginstitute.stanford.edu/montgo mery-bus-boycott
- National Park Service, Rosa Parks: https://www.nps.gov/features/malu/feat0002/wof/Rosa_Parks.htm
- National Archives, 19th Amendment to the U.S. Constitution: https://www.archives.gov/milestone-documents/19th-amendment

National Park Service, Suffragist vs. Suffragette: https://www.nps.gov/articles/suffragistvs suffragette.htm

Four-Box Reset

The Four-Box Reset is my synthesis. It grows out of the older inbox/outbox pattern I used, the spirit of the Serenity Prayer, and practical problem-solving traditions.

The four boxes are:

- Act now
- Prepare
- Connect or delegate
- Park or release

This should not be cited as a published clinical protocol. It should be described as this book's tool for sorting actions, preparations, supports, and releases.

Related source roots:

- Skills for Psychological Recovery, information gathering, prioritizing assistance, action planning, problem solving, and healthy connections. Problem-solving therapy and behavioral activation traditions.

Direct-Risk Resources

Direct-risk material changes over time and across locations. That is why this book directs readers to current resources rather than attempting to serve as a legal, medical, crisis, immigration, workplace, protest, or digital-security authority. Use the Current Resources page for these topics.

Sources to cite or recheck near publication:

- ACLU Know Your Rights:
- https://www.aclu.org/know-your-rights ACLU Protesters' Rights: https://www.aclu.org/know-your-rights/protesters-rights ACLU LGBTQ rights tracker: https://www.aclu.org/legislative-attacks-on-lgbtq-rights-2026
- EFF Surveillance Self-Defense: https://ssd.eff.org/ NNEDV Safety Net Project: https://nnedv.org/content/technology-safety/
- Safety Net: https://www.techsafety.org/ EEOC Filing A Charge of Discrimination: https://www.eeoc.gov/filing-charge-discrimination
- LawHelp.org: https://www.lawhelp.org/ National Immigration Legal Services Directory: https://www.immigrationadvocates.org/legaldirectory/
- National Disability Rights Network:
- https://www.ndrn.org/ Movement Advancement Project LGBTQ Equality Maps: https://mapresearch.org/equality/

A Final Note On Sources

Research can guide us. It can keep us honest. It can help us avoid pretending that private wisdom is sufficient. But the purpose of this book is not to overwhelm the reader with proof. Rather, it is to offer help that is grounded, modest, and usable.

www.ingramcontent.com/pod-product-compliance
Lightning Source LLC
LaVergne TN
LVHW100730061126
851857LV00011B/468